To AL —

BEING RESILIENT MEANS
NOT ONLY SURVIVING A
FAILURE, BUT ALSO LEARNING
FROM IT.

Paul

"If you like working with no nonsense people and can handle the outright truth about your business, your team, or yourself, you will love Paul Glover's *WorkQuake*™. Paul has an uncanny way of giving you the unabridged truth about your business that you need to hear."

—Douglas W. York
President, Ewing Irrigation Products, Inc.

"Glover has done a brilliant job of describing the tribulations and challenges in today's work environment—points that are critical for any manager to lead a successful organization in today's climate. *WorkQuake*™ has revolutionized and inspired countless class discussion in the two courses I teach: Management and Entrepreneurship. Glover truly understands and clearly explains how the recent economy has impacted the internal and external dynamics of management and organizations. *WorkQuake*™ is a must-read for every individual interested in management and organizational behavior."

—Todd Mertz
Business Instructor, Neuqua Valley High School

"If you want the unvarnished truth about you and your organization—and can handle it—Paul Glover is the person to give it to you. With his direct approach, unique insight into the evolving workplace and his ability to identify and solve individual and organizational issues, Paul is able to assist leaders and organizations to move to the next level of performance."

—Karen Timmons
Former CEO, Joint Commission International

"*WorkQuake*™ is an easy to read quick reference guide or 'voice on your shoulder' perfect for anyone newly promoted into a supervisory role or running a small business."

—Patrick Bye
President, Energy Dynamics, Inc.

"An absolutely entertaining and fresh perspective that is relevant to the workplace of today! Paul Glover's *WorkQuake*™ speaks in a language that everybody will relate to regardless of where they come from, what their background is, or their level of work experience. *WorkQuake*™ is a great reminder to senior leadership that they cannot ignore that people are our #1 asset, and we have to get better at managing. Organizations no longer have the choice to maintain a process that isn't useful in terms of workforce development and Paul shows us that we have got to behave differently if we are going to get competitive again. Anyone who is responsible for getting their job done through other people needs to read this book and will appreciate Paul's style of writing and sense of humor which pulls you in and keeps you reading!"

—Carol L. McClement
President, Green Light Consulting, Inc.

"... [Paul] builds learning environments that both excite and challenge ... [he] blends the wide workplace experience of an attorney and consultant, skill as an adult educator, and the vision of a seasoned administrator. Where Paul is invited to serve, he will make a major contribution."

—Richard Walsh, Ph.D
Director, Master of Arts in Organizational Leadership,
Lewis University

"Paul has been one of our primary faculty members or one who is a member of our "A Team."...I have personally learned from Paul in our conversations as well as classroom visits and have a great respect for him."

—Charles R. Sprague
College Campus Chair for Undergraduate Business and
Management, University of Phoenix

WORK QUAKE™

MAKING THE SEISMIC SHIFT TO A
"KNOWLEDGE ECONOMY"

BY PAUL GLOVER

Round Table Companies
1670 Valencia Way
Mundelein, IL 60060

www.roundtablepress.com
www.roundtablecompanies.com

The Writers of the Round Table Press name and logo are trademarks of Round Table Companies.

Executive Editor: Corey Michael Blake
Editor: Bob Yehling
Production Manager: Erin Cohen
Digital Distribution: David C. Cohen
Cover Design: Nathan Brown
Interior Design/Layout, Back Cover: Sunny DiMartino
Proofreading: Rita Hess
Last Looks: Mary Laine

Printed in Canada

First Edition: October 2011
10   9   8   7   6   5   4   3   2   1

Library of Congress Control Number: 2011938734

Library of Congress Cataloging-in-Publication Data

Glover, Paul.
WorkQuake™ / Paul Glover.—1st ed. p. cm.
ISBN 978-1-61066-022-8
1. Business Leadership. 2. Business Management. I. Title.

"To my Father, without his shared knowledge and wisdom about work and the workplace this book would never have been written."

INTRODUCTION

I Call Bullshit!

Why I Wrote This Book: As a part of the coaching process, I asked the CEO of a $30 million company to have his management team evaluate his leadership skill set.

The CEO asked his management team to be as honest as possible and to identify those areas of his leadership skill set that needed improvement.

The management team scored the CEO as "needs a lot of improvement" in four of ten areas. The CEO was genuinely shocked upon receiving this information. We then discussed an action plan to improve his performance in those areas where his scores were lowest.

The next day the CEO asked if I would send the evaluation to the management team again.

I asked him if he had a good reason for doing this and he responded, "I told my managers I was unhappy with the results of the evaluation, so we were going to do it again and this time we were going to get it right!"

That's when I "fired" him.

WorkQuake™ Wisdom: Lots of people in leadership positions give lip service to the concepts required for success in the WorkQuake™ of the Knowledge Economy - fairness, respect, engagement, honesty—but lip service doesn't cut it anymore. What does matter is behavior and action that makes those concepts a reality. And we need more of that behavior and action!

Why You Should Read This Book

Over a twenty-five year period (OMG! Has it really been that long?) of business and executive coaching and crisis management, implementing the difficult process of organizational restructuring that is forced upon failing businesses, and conducting training and development programs, I have had ample opportunity to witness the ingenuity of the human mind when it comes to inventing excuses and devising rationalizations that lead to sinking ships and destroyed businesses and lives (see the story above). While such non-productive behavior could exist in the Command & Control Industrial Economy, it cannot be tolerated in the WorkQuake™ of the Knowledge Economy (see page 1 for a definition of the WorkQuake™).

Unfortunately, this debilitating and destructive status quo behavior is firmly entrenched in the work environment and continues to cripple companies by de-motivating employees and destroying performance. Ultimately, this negative behavior causes the organization to become unprofitable and unstable. Then, if the will to survive remains among the decision makers, the company requires restructuring—a painful, but necessary survival induced process. If the will to survive has been worn down by negative behavior, then the company will stagger along, until the next economic downturn or a competitor puts it out of its misery. Thus, the reason for this book: **to call bullshit on the excuses people at all levels of an organization have for not being productive, effective and accountable participants in the Knowledge Economy Work Environment!** And I am interested in not only exposing bullshit and its detrimental effects on the work environment, but also in making practical recommendations about how to eliminate the bullshit and replace it with processes that work so companies and their employees don't have to face restructuring or their demise.

And in response to that unspoken question you have, which is, "Why should I read anything you write about improving me, my organization and the work environment?" I'll give you three answers:

1: You are feeling the effects of the WorkQuake™ and know you and your organization need help to be successful in the Work Environment of the Knowledge Economy.

2: I have the extensive experience, knowledge and practical expertise to provide the help you need to not only survive but to thrive in the Knowledge Economy.

3: If you get nothing of value from this book, you get your money back—no questions asked! Just contact me at complaints@workquake.com, arrange for return of the book and your purchase price will be sent back to you (hope you like a lot of pennies).

How is that for eliminating the bullshit?

Who should read this book?

- Anyone running one of the 85% of American companies that are not high performing organizations, but want to be - even if it means dragging most of the company kicking and screaming into the Knowledge Economy.

- Every Front Line Leader who is working "in the trenches" getting stuff done at one of the 85% of American companies that are not high performing organizations, but want to be - even if it means dragging most of the company kicking and screaming into the Knowledge Economy.

- Everyone who thinks they are in the top 15% of high performing companies, but doesn't have the profitability, culture or innovative approach to growing their business that supports their claim.

- Every Leader, at every level of the company, who realizes survival in the WorkQuake™ of the Knowledge Economy, requires eradication of Command and Control and treating employees as Partners.

- Anyone who realizes their own performance and the performance of their company can and must be improved.

- Anyone who doesn't want to see me arrive at their company to begin the restructuring process.

Who should not read this book?

- CEOs of Fortune 500 companies – I mean, seriously, if they spend their time reading this book who will save the universe?

- Theorists – I love theory as much as the next business geek, but this is a "how to book" not a "why book."

- Anyone working in the 15% of all American companies that are already high performance organizations. Why waste your time reading this book, when you should be writing one of your own and telling the rest of us how you do it?

- Anyone who remembers the "good old days" of command and control with fondness and longs for their return.

- Anyone who is not committed to improving the way work is done and how people are treated in the work environment.

- Anyone who believes they and their organization are as good as they can get.

- Anyone who wants to meet me face-to-face when I begin the restructuring or dismantling process at their company. And you don't really want to do that!

Every leader at every level of the organization needs to accept the fact that the available screwing-off time has been used up. So, begin reading and start changing the way you and your organization do business—or be prepared to get swallowed up by the WorkQuake™. But don't start reading until I tell you …

How You Should Read This Book (kinda bossy aren't I?)

As much as I would like to think this book is so well written and entertaining that it is a real page turner which you can read it cover to cover, the reality is don't do that unless you suffer from insomnia! Here is how I recommend you use/read this book:

1: When you have an operational performance issue, read *The Bottom Line* articles that gives you recommendations about how to resolve that issue. Example: If you are having a communication issue, read *The Bottom Line* articles on how to communicate better with the workforce (I know you are a great communicator, so why would you read this topic? No reason, except everyone else thinks you're a crappy communicator!). Since all of the recommendations in *The Bottom Line* articles are based on my 25 years of experience advising companies about how to improve operational performance and they actually make sense and work, it will be like having your own management consultant on-call! Not bad for a measly few bucks!

2: When you have a personal performance or productivity issue, read *The Morning Mantra* articles that contains the information you need to improve your personal performance and productivity. Example: To hold effective meetings, read *The Morning Mantra* articles about how to hold effective meetings (and, yes, I also know you are a great Meeting Master, so why would you read this topic? No reason, except everyone else thinks your meetings are a complete waste of time!). And this invaluable personal productivity information is yours absolutely FREE since you have already paid a paltry sum for *The Bottom Line* articles, so you get a twofer—pay for one and get two! And we all like twofers, don't we?

So, check out the Table of Contents, read about a topic that will help you improve your organization or your Personal Productivity and then start implementing the recommendations contained in the articles! You can thank me by buying copies of the book for those leaders and organizations (and you know who they are) who could use some help so they, too, can survive the WorkQuake™ of the Knowledge Economy.

TABLE OF CONTENTS

THE BOTTOM LINE

$\underset{\underline{\text{THE}}}{\text{BOTTOM}}$ LINE

WORKQUAKE™

What is The WorkQuake™ of the Knowledge Economy?

"Fasten your seat belts, it's going to be a bumpy ride!"
—Bette Davis in *All About Eve*

The Knowledge Economy (based on technological innovations) is the latest stage of economic development, following the Agricultural (farming) and the Industrial (manufacturing) Economies. While Agricultural and Industrial Economy employees work primarily with their hands and produce goods or services, Knowledge Economy employees work with their minds, producing ideas, generating innovation and continually improving organizational processes and systems by creative problem solving, all to better achieve an organization's goals.

WorkQuake™ – A convulsion in the world of work, caused by a shift in the fundamentals of an economy, rendering the business world and work environment virtually unrecognizable to those working in the transition period between an old economy and its replacement economy. The current WorkQuake™ is occurring between the Industrial Economy and the Knowledge Economy.

Why should you pay any attention to this phenomenon? Because you are not only living in the worst WorkQuake™ of the last 100 years, but you will continue to experience its upheavals for the rest of your life! So, fasten your seat belts, read the rest of this book and the ride won't be quite as bumpy!

Because human capital is a key component of value in the Knowledge Economy, new ideas of how to interact in the workplace environment are required if leaders and managers are to sufficiently engage Knowledge Economy employees. And such engagement is mandatory if an organization wants to thrive in the Knowledge Economy.

THE BOTTOM LINE

COMMAND AND CONTROL

Command and Control Is Alive and Well

"You can't command people to do their best; they can only command that of themselves." —Bob Nelson

Just when I think companies are truly—if reluctantly—giving up Command and Control management, along comes "the Great Recession," and Command and Control once again rears its destructive head! But why not? In times of uncertainty, when companies are experiencing situations beyond their control (i.e., massive loss of business and profit), they seek to regain control over the business, and the easiest way to achieve that goal is to assert control over those who have no choice but to accept it: their employees.

The problem with this reversion back to Command and Control management is that employees are going to remember being treated like children and resent it for a long time, and that damages long-term productivity and loyalty. While the overriding temptation is to respond to any crisis by becoming Theory X managers, who believe employees must be forced to work, my strong recommendation is to resist temptation and continue to treat employees like adults who have something to contribute and are valued members of the company's team.

Here are some signs that Command and Control may be creeping back into the company:

1: There is an "I" in Team.
Employees are no longer involved or included in the decision making process, and supervisors and managers are making all operational decisions.

2: "If I want your opinion, I'll give it to you."
No one is listening to employees' ideas and opinions about how to improve the operation and survive the current crisis.

3: "You can't handle the truth."
Information about the condition of the company is withheld because employees don't need to know or might cry if they knew the truth.

4: "The sky is falling!"
Supervisors and managers are constantly freaking out, taking away any sense of security and offering little hope for the future.

5: "You are lucky you still have a job."
Supervisors and managers stop recognizing and rewarding "above and beyond" performance because they think employees are lucky to have jobs and tell them that.

6: "We can't afford no stinkin' Training and Developing Programs."
The company stops any training and developing programs, which makes "doing more with less, but doing it better!" difficult for employees to achieve.

Command and Control management needs to vanish, not because of human nature (which dictates that we control every situation), but because the workforce will no longer tolerate being treated like children. To thrive in the Knowledge Economy, companies need employees who are capable of innovation, creativity and commitment to the company's vision. Companies certainly won't receive that long-term behavior by reverting back to Command and Control techniques during this or any other economic crisis.

COMMUNICATION

The Boss's Memorandum to the Entire Company

"Even the frankest and bravest of subordinates do not talk with their boss the same way they talk with colleagues."
—Robert Greenleaf

To: My Direct Reports and Anyone Else in the Company Who Has to Interact With Me

From: The Boss

Re: How to Interact With Me Most Effectively

I realize I am often not clear in expressing my expectations for the operation and for you. To help remedy this situation, improve the company and make the operation run more smoothly, here are some guidelines on how I would like you to interact with me. These guidelines are just suggestions, but I believe they will improve our relationship and help the company operate at a higher level:

Communication: (fill in the blank)

Decision Making and Problem Solving: (fill in the blank)

Teamwork: (fill in the blank)

Conflict Resolution: (fill in the blank)

Time Management: (fill in the blank)

When we are working together, do not hesitate to let me know what additional information about me would help us work together more productively.

—THE BOSS

This is the memorandum I want every executive to prepare and disseminate to the entire company. Why? Because most bosses, at every level of the organization, believe they are perfectly clear about their expectations, how they work and how they want others to interact with them. However, the reality is: not so much! Many bosses believe employees who interact with them to get work done are telepathic—they can read the boss's mind! Because employees have learned that most bosses react adversely when asked to clarify or explain the incoherent request or order they just issued, most employees don't ask for any clarification or explanation; they just hope (never a good solution!) they understand enough of the message to get the job done. Or, they speak to the boss's assistant who, because of familiarity with the boss's "unique" brand of communication, is able to interpret what the boss wants done.

Not only will this memorandum help employees understand how to best interact with the boss, but it also helps the boss examine and become aware of his or her own shortcomings in these critical areas and, hopefully, to work at overcoming them. This may also stop the boss from rolling his or her eyes, glancing towards Heaven or silently asking God why they were cursed with such a stupid employee. This gesture is seldom lost on the employee, confirming to them the risk taken by merely asking a clarifying question. It also ensures they won't ask again.

So, write the memorandum already!

THE BOTTOM LINE

COMMUNICATION

Can You Hear Me Now?

*"To effectively communicate, we must realize that we are all
different in the way we perceive the world and use this
understanding as a guide to our communication with others."*
—Anthony Robbins

During these tough economic times, I assisted Doug, the president of a $300 million national distribution company, in preparing a crucial presentation to 350 managers assembled for the company's annual meeting. Doug realized the global economic meltdown, as well as recent company downsizing, significantly raised the anxiety level among the company's employees and a critical part of his job as the leader was not only to set the company's course, but also maintain employee morale and focus by clearly communicating that course. Through his presentation, Doug exercised exemplary leadership by answering the employees' spoken and unspoken questions about the company's future.

Doug gets it. In tough times, it is essential for leaders at all levels of a company to engage in a dialogue with employees about the employees' future with the company.

Yet, 46% of leaders take no action to communicate with the workforce to address anxiety in the workplace! This failure to communicate makes me very angry. It is never easy to tell employees bad news, but failing to communicate the bad news is worse because it is a failure of leadership. It leaves employees susceptible to the rumor mill, and that crushes productivity. Employees wonder if their jobs are safe and begin checking Monster.com for available job opportunities.

Being a leader at any level requires you perform both the easy and hard tasks—and everything in between—for the good of the organization and the people who support it. Whether you are a Front Line Leader or the CEO, you have an obligation to communicate with your employees, especially when there is uncertainty in the workplace. To ensure your organization isn't within the 46% of non-communicating companies, follow these eight recommendations about how to communicate with the workforce:

1: Develop a Formal Communication Program.

Without a formalized communication program setting forth the "hows" and "whens" of communicating with employees, adequate communication is seldom accomplished—especially during a crisis. Make sure everyone from the CEO to the Front Line Leader knows about whatever situation needs to be discussed, as well as what to communicate to the workforce. There is nothing more frustrating to a Front Line Leader than to find out about a situation from a member of his work team.

2: Be Constantly Visible in the Workplace.

Visibility in the workplace is a vital form of verbal and non-verbal communication. Being visible reassures and allows for informal dialogue with employees. This doesn't mean just having formal meetings with the workforce. Place yourself where the employees are, and join in the informal discussions that take place at daily kick-off or sales meetings. Sit down with different lunch groups. Show up on every shift—even the hoot owl shift—and in every department. Some will ask, "Isn't this a huge time commitment?" The answer: Yes, it is! But it is a *necessary and worthwhile time commitment* all good leaders make if their company is going to thrive.

3: Be in Front of the Rumor Mill.

Rumors destroy morale and productivity. While rumors can't be eliminated, their effects can be controlled. An established communication program allows management to discover what rumors are circulating and respond to them quickly so they do as little damage as possible.

4: Acknowledge Emotions.
Circumstances may cause employees to be disillusioned, worried and angry. The sooner you acknowledge these emotions, the better. Consider what employees need to hear, (such as what they have lost or are afraid they will lose), not just what you want to say, and address the issues they will discuss when you leave the room.

5: Inform the Team.
You don't want employees jumping to the wrong conclusions because they aren't receiving adequate and accurate information from the company. Don't assume employees know what you know or that they need to know everything. Give employees the information they need so they understand the situation as it affects them, including bad news, without alarming them unnecessarily. Employees are adults and can handle bad news. To treat them otherwise damages the trust and respect existing between the employees and the company.

6: Create a Dialogue, Not a Monologue.
Make your communication two-way. Ask for feedback and questions and mean it! Giving employees the opportunity to talk and ask questions will make them feel better. Their questions will also reveal their concerns, tell you what they are really thinking and identify rumors so you can quickly respond to them. It is okay to say you don't know the answer but will find out and get back to the person who asked the question—as long as you do get back to them!

7: Issue a Call to Action and Share Hope.
To communicate bad news successfully, articulate a Plan of Action explaining the current situation and the hope for the future. Be clear about what the workforce can do to help. Good employees want to be involved in helping the company, and they need to know where to focus their energy.

8: Follow Up.

Once is never enough! Just because the company initially communicates with its workforce about how the company is doing doesn't mean communication with the workforce is complete. Employees who hear bad news about the economy every day need to know the status of the company on an ongoing basis. Otherwise, they will rely on the rumor mill for their information—and that "information" will always be worse than the truth. Keep communicating with updates and answers.

Every company needs to develop a formal and informal communication program that provides information in good times and bad, so the people you count on to help solve the company's problems know what those problems are and how they can help solve them. A leader's primary obligation to the workforce and the company is to communicate! Communicate! Communicate!

Time to Stop the Socialist Pay Raise

"My belief is firm in a law of compensation. The true rewards
are ever in proportion to the labour and sacrifices made."
—Nikola Tesla

The ongoing tremors of the WorkQuake™ of the Knowledge Economy means actions that worked in the past will not work effectively now—such as how people are paid! Companies must look at their compensation program with new eyes. In 2010, the median annual pay raise was 2.5%. In 2011, it is anticipated to be 3%. Employers everywhere are patting themselves on the back, congratulating themselves for a job well done. After all, in a crappy economy, any opportunity to give increases in wages will thrill the workforce and strengthen the bond of loyalty between employees and the organization, right?

My response: Not as much as you think.

Do employers seriously believe a paltry 3% increase will satisfy employees? Of course, employees are not going to turn down any increase, and they are going to express their gratitude in front of management. After all, jobs are scarce. Any sign of dismay at the fact the annual 3% increase doesn't even cover the increase in the price of a Starbucks coffee could turn an employee into a victim in the next round of layoffs! Workers will continue to publicly announce their gratitude for the company's seeming largesse. However, the Core Employees will be mad and they will have given one more reason to take a hike when the job market improves.

Why would Core Employees be upset at the 3% company-wide increase? Because they can't understand why *everyone* in the organization should get a raise! To the workforce, it is readily apparent who deserves a raise and who doesn't, but they are never asked for their opinion, are they? Any wage increase is decided at the executive level and passed down to the peons who staff the front lines. The only explanation? "This is all we can afford this year." Implicit within that statement is "and you are damned lucky we are doing such a good job managing this company that you still have a job and we can afford to give you any increase at all."

I come at compensation from an entirely different direction. I think it is time for leaders to rethink the annual 3% giveaway—a giveaway because the company gets exactly nothing in return for this waste of company assets.

As I have previously stated, nobody is impressed or motivated with a 3% increase. After the second paycheck, this small increase is viewed as "what I'm paid to show up." My contention, backed up with some science, is that to get the employees' attention, a company needs to offer at least a 10% annual compensation increase. An increase of less than 10% won't lead to greater employee effort to improve business results. Of course, there is growing evidence that no amount of money will make an employee care about the job, but that is another topic.

My question to company leaders: What is the point of giving everybody a raise when there are employees (The Others) in every organization who merit no increase whatsoever? There is no ROI in giving The Others any increase in pay, since that only rewards poor performance behavior. Especially when this unmerited raise takes money away from the Core Employees, who, by definition, are performing "above and beyond" established expectations. Of course, I can hear the howls from HR that we have to give everybody something; otherwise, "they" will cause trouble. My response: man up and tell them to bring it on! Unless an employee deserves a raise for doing something other than taking up space and air, then the company should give them nothing! Think about the benefits of taking the money that goes to The Others and giving it to the Core Employees. Instead of a 3% raise, you could increase their compensation by 10%—a meaningful, impactful raise that may generate loyalty if not motivation. Finally, let the Front Line Leaders, who know who is really doing the work, be deeply involved in the decision as to who gets the dough!

Also, since we are constantly talking about increased performance as the Holy Grail, shouldn't companies finally align compensation with performance? Certainly, organizations need to benchmark against the marketplace to ensure their pay is competitive; otherwise, they will not attract talent and could lose their best workers to a higher paying competitor. But after determining an employee's base pay is equitable, then any increase should be entirely performance-based bonuses and paid on a (gasp!) monthly basis! I would have recommended weekly payment of bonuses, since to align pay with performance, the connection between the two needs to be as close in time as possible. However, I didn't want to give the payroll department a massive group heart attack. Seriously, is it really that hard to cut a bonus check each week? And is it really so hard to determine, by measuring actual performance, who deserves a bonus each week? I think not.

Yes, eliminating the one size-fits-all compensation concept is tough work, but if organizations are really ready to stop giving lip service to performance-based pay, then it's time to eliminate the Socialist Pay Raise and start really rewarding performance in a meaningful and comprehensive fashion.

$\underset{\text{LINE}}{\overset{\text{BOTTOM}}{\text{THE}}}$ 06

Why Would We Really All Want to Get Along?

"Conflict cannot be eliminated. It can only be managed."
—Anonymous

I love conflict and confrontation! As a "recovering" trial attorney, I am trained to view conflict as the natural course of events when the ideas and interests of two or more individuals or groups clash—which, in a vibrant organization, they should be doing all the time. This clash creates the tension necessary for constructive organizational change. Without effectively managed workplace conflict, the organization cannot progress because the unchallenged status quo will eventually stifle individual creativity and organizational growth.

The reason most leaders hate conflict, and try to avoid it at all cost, is that they don't understand its value to the organization, and they haven't been trained in managing constructive conflict. Workplace conflict management is a skill set that can turn potentially destructive disputes into opportunities to make the organization more productive and efficient and convert conflict into creative answers to difficult workplace issues.

All leaders are required to deal with two types of workplace conflict:

Good Conflict: People respectfully disagreeing and the tension this creates encourages the free flow of ideas, creativity and productive activities.

Bad Conflict: Unresolved conflict that breeds in an atmosphere of tension, misunderstanding and fear and creates:

- Employee dissatisfaction

- Diminished production

- Poor customer service

- Employee turnover

- Increased absenteeism

- Increased employee stress

To understand how to respond to bad conflict in the workplace, leaders need to be aware of the following root causes of conflict:

Denial – some people do not or will not see a conflict

Skill Deficiencies – employees who are poor communicators or poor negotiators

Lack of Information – caused by poor organizational communication processes

Conflicting Interests – different wants and needs of those involved in the conflict

Stress – 10–20% of the workforce suffers from stress

Personality Style – some personalities will clash

Scarce Resources – more work and less resources (time, people, material, money)

Organizational Deficiencies – no organizational system exists to resolve issues

Selfishness – greed causes conflict

Evil Intent – willful intent to cause harm

Fear – usually of the unknown and fueled by rumors and gossip

Once leaders understand the nature of bad conflict and realize it requires their involvement, they can use the following eight steps to manage conflicts:

1: Define the conflict.
Determine the real reason for the conflict before attempting to devise a resolution.

2: It's not you versus me; it's you and me versus the problem.
Conflict management must be based on "collaboration" not "competition."

3: Find common ground.
Establish areas of agreement by identifying shared concerns before moving to any areas of disagreement.

4: Separate opinions from facts.
Facts help clarify perceptions, which helps to resolve conflict.

5: Have an open mind.
There are always at least two sides to every conflict. Pre-determining the outcome before hearing all sides is not permitted.

6: Listen actively.
Listen with the intent to understand, not respond.

7: Silence is not necessarily assent.

If there is no clearly defined, affirmatively accepted resolution to the conflict, there is no resolution.

8: Follow up.

To ensure the conflict is resolved, follow up with the parties involved to determine if the resolution is working.

Finally, here are the prevalent myths about workplace conflict that prevent effective conflict management:

"Just ignore it and it will go away" – conflict needs to be addressed as soon as it appears.

"There must be a winner and a loser" – compromise is essential, but only possible if there is mutual respect.

"Every conflict can be resolved" – sometimes the best resolution possible is to learn to live with an ongoing disagreement.

By honing their conflict management skill set using the process set forth, leaders will become more effective at resolving workplace conflict. And don't argue with me about this!

THE BOTTOM LINE

CONTINUOUS OPERATIONAL PERFORMANCE IMPROVEMENT

Kaizen

"Continuous effort—not strength or intelligence—is the key to unlocking our potential." —Winston Churchill

I am a confirmed Starbucks addict. Because the burnt flavor of their beans titillates my taste buds in just the right way, at 5:00 every morning I walk to my neighborhood Starbucks and kick-start my day with a whole milk grande latte, no foam, extra shot. Makes my mouth water just thinking about it!

One morning, as the barista was preparing my latte, I noticed that instead of shots of espresso from the espresso machine pouring directly into shot glasses, the coffee was going into the cardboard drinking cup. When I asked the barista where the shot glasses were, he responded that Starbucks had determined the coffee residue—called "crema"—that remained in the shot glass should go into the drinking cup since it gives the coffee a sweeter, fuller taste. In other words, it would increase the quality of the product and also save up to five seconds of time for each drink made (I looked that up). As I left Starbucks, I thought, "What a great example of the Japanese philosophy of *kaizen*!"

Kaizen (Japanese for "improvement" or "change for the better") is a philosophy focused upon continuous improvement through the ongoing examination of standardized work processes and elimination of waste. It was made famous by Toyota before that company imploded when it stopped following the principle. Properly applied, *kaizen* leads to continual improvement in productivity and quality. Starbucks was founded in 1971. Four decades later, this very successful company is still engaged in making small changes to its products and operation to improve its products and service.

Can you say the same about your company? Are you and your employees engaged in a daily quest to improve the operation? Or are you satisfied with doing things the way they have always been done because that's the easy way?

In the WorkQuake™ of the Knowledge Economy, you and your employees need to be continually engaged in Continuous Operational Performance Improvement—to improve the company's products, services and business operations at all levels. Why? Because in the Knowledge Economy, success is never final (just ask Toyota!), and the core reason anyone's job exists is to continually make the company better.

CONTINUOUS OPERATIONAL PERFORMANCE IMPROVEMENT

Stop Trying to Teach the Pig to Dance!

"When his life was ruined, his family killed, his farm destroyed, Job knelt down on the ground and yelled up to the heavens, 'Why god? Why me?' and the thundering voice of God answered, 'There's just something about you that pisses me off.'" —Stephen King

My father was a farmer, a blacksmith and an electrician who worked the hoot owl shift at a General Motors plant to pay for his farming addiction. He was also a pragmatist. After observing me engaged in a passionate argument with a person who clearly was not listening to what I said and did not intend to change his position, he told me, "Stop trying to teach the pig to dance." Perplexed by this farm wisdom, I asked why. He replied, "It's a waste of your time and it irritates the pig."

As usual, he was right.

This quote did not originate with my dad, but it illustrates how you should be dealing with The Others. I don't believe The Others will ever improve their performance, regardless of how much time, energy and resources a company expends on them. Which leads to an interesting question: how much time, energy and resources does the average company invest in The Others in an attempt to improve their performance? My best estimate, based on responses to that question in my Front Line

Leader workshops, is companies spend 80% of their total employee management time on The Others and the more problematic Temporary Employees—and only 20% of their time coaching and training the best of the work force, the Core Employees and those Temporary Employees who have the potential to become Core Employees! This is truly ass backwards (another farm saying used by my father)!

Companies are able to engage in Continuous Operational Performance Improvement only if they concentrate on increasing their strengths and eliminating their weaknesses. Core Employees and the top 30% of the Temporary Employees are the company's strength. Leaders need to flip the percentages I cited in the previous paragraph. They need to invest 80% of their time in training, coaching, praising and rewarding Core Employees and Temporary Employees who have the potential to become Core Employees so they will become Core Employees. When that goal is achieved, the remaining 20% of their time needs to be focused on removing The Others from the company.

How much time is your company spending on trying to rehabilitate The Others? Wouldn't that time be better spent further strengthening and increasing the value of Core and high performing Temporary Employees?

DECISION MAKING

Decision Making: Just Do It!

"To succeed, jump as quickly at opportunities as you do at conclusions." —Benjamin Franklin

What is the difference between "making a decision" and "jumping to a conclusion"? Making a decision requires you have the appropriate accurate data to support the decision, while jumping to a conclusion is based solely on emotions. No company survives for long with decisions based solely on emotions!

I just returned from a visit with a client, who I have been assisting in an organizational restructuring process. During a twelve-month period, this process required two non-profitable operations out of five total operations be eliminated, expenses be reduced significantly and half the management team to be replaced because of their failure to meet performance standards. All of these difficult decisions were made based on data that fully supported each decision. However, on this visit I was unpleasantly surprised when the management team informed me they had decided to purchase an expensive piece of equipment, not based on any data to support the purchase, but rather based on the hope they had that if they purchased the equipment, it would generate the ROI required to support the cost of the equipment.

I immediately called a time out and explained for the twelfth time in twelve months that "hope is never a solution" and the "if you build it, they will come" attitude means "they" will be coming to the company's liquidation sale! Everyone looked properly abashed. The proponents of the purchase promised to have the data supporting the purchase available at our next meeting.

This example highlights the propensity most leaders have to jump to a conclusion to justify a decision. This is the easiest way to get what we want without having to go to the trouble of showing any rational reason for making the decision. It is the "I want it because I want it!" method of decision making. It's also one of the quickest ways for a company to self-destruct. Companies can avoid this destructive method of decision making by:

1: Realizing intuition does count when making a decision—but only if there is sufficient experience with similar situations to support the intuition. Also, intuition works best in a stable environment, but not so much in a changing environment.

2: Encouraging dissent in the decision making process.

3: Avoiding "group think" by having a diverse and competent collective intelligence involved in the decision making process.

4: Avoiding decision making when emotions (e.g., stress, anger, fear and anxiety) are running high.

5: Realizing the most obvious choice is often the right choice.

6: Ensuring that personal incentives produced by the decision are not influencing the process.

7: Avoiding analysis paralysis. At some point, enough data has been collected to make a decision. To say "I need more time" after that point is reached is a stalling tactic that becomes detrimental, because:

a: By delaying a decision, you allow anxiety to build up.

b: By delaying a decision, you allow the decision to get bigger and harder than it really is.

c: By delaying a decision, you create an energy suck for the entire period of the delay.

Now that you are aware of the decision making rules, don't just think about what you want to do, decide to do it—the right way!

THE BOTTOM LINE

10

DISCIPLINE AND DISCHARGE

Your Company Is Not the Marine Corps!

"No man is left behind." —U.S. Marine Corps

The motto "No man is left behind" is one of The Marine Corps' core beliefs and helps make the organization a world-class fighting machine. While I applaud the Marine Corps for the *esprit de corps* it exhibits in standing by the principle of "no man is left behind," it is not a principle any company that wants to thrive in the WorkQuake™ of the Knowledge Economy should attempt to apply to its workforce. Nonetheless, I am constantly amazed by how many companies believe they have to "save" every employee, even though the employee in question has proven repeatedly to be one of the unproductive "Others"—the 20% of the workforce who should have been fired yesterday.

Of course, the "no man is left behind" concept assumes the company even acknowledges the fact that its workforce includes underperformers. Often, when I point out to a new client that 20% of their workforce is comprised of The Others, the immediate response is, "That may be the case at other companies, but it is not the case at our company!" I then challenge the client to hold a focus group with Front Line Leaders (supervisors and Core Employees) to discuss how to improve the company. During that discussion, each participant is asked to rank the employees in their work group as "Core" (the 20% of the workforce hardwired to give 100% whether they want to or not), "Temporary" (the 60% of the workforce constantly deciding whether to be a Core Employee or one of The Others) and The Others (employees who should have been fired yesterday). Explain this is the beginning of a performance improvement initiative, and no employee is going to get fired because of this placement process; otherwise, Front Line Leaders might be reluctant to properly place some employees. Since they observe them in the workplace every day, Front Line Leaders will quickly identify the Core Employees and The Others. If a Front Line Leader can't quickly make this placement, or if they list all their Employees as Core Employees, that leader's effectiveness needs to be seriously evaluated and he or she needs training in evaluating employee performance!

Once the dirty little secret about the existence of The Others is out in the open, the Front Line Leaders and the Core Employees will expect something to be done about it (Awareness + Knowledge = an Expectation of Action) since they are very tired of tolerating and picking up the slack for The Others! Be forewarned that if you solicit the Front Line Leaders in this placement process but fail to take action, you will generate dissatisfaction among those involved in the process. The ripple effect will cause other Front Line Leaders to be suspicious of any involvement in the placement process when you ask them to participate. I suggest developing Individual Performance Improvement Action Plans for each employee, based on a dialogue that determines the actions the employee needs to take to increase their level of performance and what the company needs to do to assist them. This approach, which generates buy-in from those employees who want to improve, will create job satisfaction for Core Employees and the opportunity for Temporary Employees and The Others (even though I seriously doubt it will happen!) to become Core Employees. While The Others should not be tolerated in the workforce (a culture of excellence cannot tolerate mediocrity), time, effort and company resources have already been expended to recruit, hire and train them. Because of this expenditure of company resources, offering The Others a final opportunity to become Core Employees makes sense.

When one of The Others fails to meet the reasonable expectations set forth in their Individual Performance Improvement Action Plan, many leaders struggle with what to do. Because of this investment of resources in The Others, managers continue to deceive themselves into believing that, with just a little more attention and training, The Others can be "saved" and will become Core Employees—or at least more productive—and that replacement employees would perform no better. Now for the reality: employees decide how productive they want to be. The obligation of the company is not to "save" employees, but rather to ensure:

- That employees know the reasonable expectations about performance and attitude when hired.

- That expectations are reinforced through frequent performance improvement and development meetings.

- That employees have the resources and training necessary to meet expectations.

- That employees are recognized and rewarded when they meet and exceed expectations.

When the company fulfills these obligations, and an employee still fails to meet expectations, they need to leave. When leaders refuse to take action and terminate The Others for failing to meet expectations, the ramifications are dramatic and immediate. Core Employees become irritated because they have to continue to carry The Others. Also, the risk of turning Temporary Employees into The Others is increased because every time a Temporary Employee sees one of The Others performing below expectations and getting away with it, it becomes *acceptable* for them to perform at that same low level.

All Leaders need to take the appropriate action to eliminate The Others from the workforce as expeditiously as possible. The Marine Corps would consider a failure to do so a dereliction of duty.

$\underset{\text{THE}}{}$ BOTTOM LINE

11

DISCIPLINE AND DISCHARGE

Discipline Fairly

"Only undertake what you can do in an excellent fashion. There are no prizes for average performance." —Brian Tracy

While I am very optimistic about the future of the Knowledge Economy workplace, I'm not an idiot. I know The Others are very adroit at sneaking into and remaining in the workplace because:

Management is susceptible to being fooled into believing the person who was just hired has the potential to become a Core Employee (a reason to have members of the work team involved in the hiring process—they are much harder to fool!) when they definitely do not. And after The Others have been hired, there is, for a variety of lame reasons, an inherent reluctance to "pull the trigger" and terminate an employee who is playing the system ("I hired him or her and if I fire him or her it will make me look bad!") when not firing them makes you look worse and hurts the organization—I'm just saying!

As long as there are The Others and Temporary Employees who may become The Others, it is necessary to have an effective and fair Disciplinary Process in place to act as a safety net. This also forces managers to play fair and not allow an undue amount of bias into the employee-employer relationship. It also forces manager and employee to focus on reasonable expectations and continual performance improvement required to meet those reasonable expectations. A properly planned and implemented Disciplinary Process will effectively and expeditiously transform The Others, who refuse to meet reasonable expectations, from employees to customers.

How do you create a Disciplinary Process that protects the company when one of The Others is terminated? By following these Eight Tips and Six Righteous Rules! While following these tips and rules may not stop the terminated employee from filing a charge of discrimination with the Equal Employment Opportunity Commission, as a "recovering" labor and employment lawyer (once a lawyer always a lawyer even if not a practicing one!), I guarantee it will stop them from winning such a charge:

Eight Tips Guaranteed to Improve the Disciplinary Process:

1: Dignity and Respect!
Since it is unavoidable that some employees will need to be disciplined or terminated based on their conduct or failure to adequately perform, the concept of *just discipline* must be the bedrock of a good company's disciplinary program. *Just discipline* is based on treating each employee with dignity and respect, regardless of the circumstances surrounding the situation causing their discipline—excluding employees who also happen to be serial killers!

2: Discipline Should Not Only Be Punishment!
The concept of discipline has changed in the Knowledge Economy. Companies should no longer be trying to only punish an employee whose conduct or performance does not meet the company's standards. Rather, through a formalized and objective progressive discipline process, the company should offer the employee an opportunity to improve and help them take that opportunity. This approach shifts the responsibility for improvement away from the company to the employee—where it belongs—and provides protection to the company from a litigious employee.

3: Progressive Discipline as a Tool for Improvement!
Properly applied progressive discipline creates a growing sense of urgency for the employee to improve performance or conduct. This happens by conveying what needs to improve in order for the employee to avoid the next step in the progressive discipline process

and rejoin the team. The keys to an effective progressive discipline process are:

Clarity: The employee knows what expectations—the levels of performance or conduct—are required.

Consistency: The applications of the rules don't change for employees because of who they are.

Communication: The leader imposing the discipline works to improve the employee's performance and conduct by providing regular feedback about improvements made through a formalized Individual Performance Improvement Plan.

4: Dotting the I's and Crossing the T's!

Effective performance improvement requires the Front Line Leader, the person who observes employees on a daily basis, to keep accurate daily records of each employee's work activities—both good and bad. This is essential for effective performance improvement reviews and for a *righteous firing*—an involuntary termination of employment that withstands the scrutiny of a governmental agency or a plaintiff's employment lawyer. Righteous firings occur when it becomes apparent an employee does not intend to change bad behaviors and refuses to improve performance. Unfortunately, most Front Line Leaders have difficulty keeping the required daily employee performance records, so when the decision is made to terminate, there is not adequate documentation to support the decision. This allows an employee who should be terminated to continue polluting the overall performance and morale of the workplace. It is essential that companies provide training so Front Line Leaders know what records they need to keep and then create the necessary forms so a record of the employee's daily activities can be easily maintained.

5: Remove Human Resources as an Obstacle to a Righteous Firing!

The Human Resources Department can become an unwarranted obstacle that Front Line Leaders have to overcome in order to remove unproductive or disruptive employees. HR's job should be to advise Front Line Leaders about policies and procedures, assure compliance with the law, ensure fairness and consistency in the disciplinary process, provide training in performance improvement techniques and serve as a watchdog so employees are treated fairly. If a Front Line Leader properly observes the established policies governing employee behavior, identifies performance and conduct issues, properly documents those issues and initiates discipline in a fair, objective manner, then HR should not attempt to second-guess a Front Line Leader's actions or attempt to stop them from getting rid of The Others. Front Line Leaders who must constantly fight HR's *"give them another chance"* mentality eventually become frustrated and, rather than fight with HR, accept the fact they must tolerate poor performers. Front Line Leaders need to be encouraged to upgrade the workforce, not tolerate the disruptive and non-productive behavior of The Others.

6: Make Every Termination a "Just Cause" Firing!

Nearly every company's employee handbook contains a dressed-up, legalese version of the following language: "YOU ARE AN AT WILL EMPLOYEE. YOU CAN BE FIRED AT ANY TIME FOR ANY REASON OR NO REASON! AND DON'T YOU FORGET IT!" While the language is not this direct, Employment at Will language often appears in BOLD type in employee handbooks and its effect is exactly the same. While the employment at will concept is alive and well in every state, do you really want your employees thinking you would fire them for *any* reason or *no* reason? Doesn't this go against everything the company says to employees about being part of the team? I recommend a better approach, one that reflects the attitude of a company dedicated to thriving in the Knowledge Economy: show your employees they are an integral part of achieving the company's goals of increased service, productivity and profit by eliminating employment at will and implementing a progressive disciplinary procedure that provides an employee can only be fired for Just Cause. This is an initially scary, but necessary, relinquishing of control that needs to be done if a company is serious about employee engagement.

7: Stop Using the Four Tendencies When Dealing with The Others!

The four tendencies most Front Line Leaders reveal when dealing with The Others are: avoiding, overreacting, complaining and lecturing. To become more effective at dealing with The Others: (1) recognize which tendencies you use; (2) realize using them does not improve or eliminate the problem; (3) STOP using the tendencies; and (4) use the Progressive Disciplinary Process to deal with The Others by either improving their performance or terminating them.

8: Stop Making the Front Line Leaders Fire People!

It's amazing how often a Front Line Leader finally terminates one of The Others and then hears, "Why did it take you so long to fire that person?" Don't kid yourself! Team members know as much, if not more, than you do about who is performing and who is not performing. They seethe in silence because The Others are allowed to continue to drag the team's performance down. A real belief in the teamwork concept and employee engagement requires the team that helps hire new employees (the team does participate in the hiring process, right?) be equally involved in the disciplinary and discharge process. By involving the team in the disciplinary and discharge process, you recognize team members are responsible for the team's overall performance, acknowledge the importance of input from team members and encourage team cohesiveness and involvement. All very good things.

The Six Righteous Rules

1: The employee must know what the rules are, and the consequences for breaking the rules. Don't play "gotcha!" with employees by being unclear about rules and expectations—it is demeaning behavior and a serious waste of time. "Gotcha" behavior undermines the concept that discipline is not punishment, but rather an attempt to improve the conduct or performance of an employee. Once the company plays "gotcha!", it has given the employees permission to also play games with the disciplinary system. The Others are experts at gaming the system—always being on the edge of termination, but never going *over* the edge. Don't validate their bad behavior by engaging in bad behavior of your own.

2: The employee must know what he or she did to violate the rule, there must be a willingness to hear the employee's side. There must be an agreement about what the employee must do to fix the problem, and there must be an agreed upon reasonable time period for the employee to attempt to fix the problem.

3: There can be no abusive behavior towards the employee during the disciplinary process. So, stop the eyeball rolling and sighing already—they see that and know exactly what it means!

4: The punishment must fit the crime. If you have just cause and have already decided to terminate an employee, stop paying lip service to progressive discipline and pull the trigger already.

5: There must be consistent application of the rules by using objectivity when investigating and resolving disciplinary issues, and by treating the offending employee as if he or she were a Core Employee who had committed the same infraction.

6: There must be an appeals process to allow a review of the discipline by a higher authority. The presence of an appeals process guarantees the integrity of the Progressive Disciplinary Process by stopping any unwarranted discipline by Front Line Leaders.

It's time to realize there is a new day in the workplace! Employees and management alike feel the changes caused by the WorkQuake™ of the Knowledge Economy with increased intensity. The old command and control methods of management, including the traditional concept of discipline and discharge, are less and less effective, and the development of new approaches, more in keeping with the requirements for success in the Knowledge Economy, must be considered. Of course, companies don't have to change. As W. Edwards Deming stated, "It is not necessary to change. Survival is not mandatory."

DISCIPLINE AND DISCHARGE

Has HR Become the 21st Century Union?

"The company made me a scapegoat, just like my three previous employers." —One of The Others

When I was a union leader (yes, I once worked for The Dark Side—and very effectively, too!), the objection most employers had about the union was not increased wages and benefits but the loss of control over their employees. Companies hated the restrictions placed on their ability to manage employees because of seniority provisions, rigid job descriptions and the grievance process that protected unproductive and disruptive employees (The Others) from discipline and discharge.

Things have changed in the twenty years since I left the union business. Union membership is below eight percent of America's workforce, and the power of the union to unreasonably restrict an employer's operation has been tempered by shrinking membership. However, the complaints of a company's Front Line Leaders haven't changed! Now, instead of complaining about the union, today's Front Line Leaders are angry because most Human Resources Departments hamper their ability to get the job done by saddling them with restrictive employee policies and procedures that protect The Others. This leads to a very legitimate question: **Has HR evolved into the Labor Union of the Knowledge Economy?**

In most instances, the attitude of the HR Department is based on the concerns of the company's lawyers. As a "recovering" lawyer, I absolutely understand the company lawyer's mindset. Lawyers want the HR Department to have as many procedures and policies in place to eliminate as much freedom of action as possible from Front Line Leaders. This is supposed to ensure that no Front Line Leader makes a mistake when it comes to dealing with an employee—especially a "difficult" employee (translation: one of The Others).

This overly restrictive control of Front Line Leaders made sense in the Industrial Economy, when Command and Control was the order of the day. At that time, the workforce needed protection from the harsh actions of Front Line Leaders, who were prejudiced and managed through intimidation and coercion. The restrictive provisions of the union contract were in response to this abusive conduct and protected the workforce from bad Front Line Leaders.

But that was back in the day! Today's successful Front Line Leaders understand diversity and are becoming more coaches than bosses. Because of these changes in the managerial mindset and the requirement that every company in the WorkQuake™ of the Knowledge Economy must compete with high performance work teams, Front Line Leaders need to have more freedom to get the job done. And this includes the ability to quickly eliminate non-productive employees from the workforce without the unreasonable restrictions placed on them by the HR Department.

By having an HR Department that functions as a union, companies are being placed at a competitive disadvantage in the WorkQuake™ of the Knowledge Economy. It's time for HR to catch up with the attitude of the rest of the workforce and become a partner, not an obstacle, to organizational productivity.

THE BOTTOM LINE

13

EMPLOYEE ENGAGEMENT

Inclusion Equals Engagement

"I can teach anybody how to get what they want out of life. The problem is that I can't find anybody who can tell me what they want." —Mark Twain

Every organization with which I work to improve employee performance struggles with the reality of employee engagement. While every leader knows that without meaningful employee engagement in the work process, at every level of the organization, the company cannot thrive in the hypercompetitive world of the Knowledge Economy, few leaders understand how to get beyond the buzzword of "empowerment" and actually engage employees in the work process.

I believe the answer is simple: give employees more control over their work by involving them in solving the problems they face. While this seems an obvious solution, the leadership workshops I conduct on Problem Solving and Decision Making inevitably reveal the difficulties involved in transferring any decision making control to employees. When I raise the necessity of including Core Employees in the decision making and problem solving process, leaders immediately reject the idea because they believe only the leaders can and should be the company's problem solvers, and that Core employees don't want to be included in problem solving.

I then ask them to consider the following:

1: They are wasting their valuable time solving problems that should be delegated to others with the skill set necessary to solve those problems. About 80% of the problems leaders face on a daily basis are routine or recurring problems that can be solved by employees. The inclusion of Core Employees in the problem solving process will lighten their workload and make them more successful leaders.

2: Including employees in the problem solving process doesn't mean leaders give up decision making authority. The workplace is not a democracy, and the final decision rests with the leaders, who must ensure the problem is solved in the best way possible under existing circumstances.

3: The leader's time is better spent resolving the remaining 20% of the issues that are stopping the organization from moving to the next level of performance (e.g., performance gaps between what is supposed to happen and what actually does happen).

4: Core Employees want to be involved in the problem solving process—but they have to be invited or coaxed into it. During the Industrial Economy, Core Employees learned their suggestions were not welcomed. My dad, a Core Employee who worked in a General Motors plant, told me, "When I punch in, they tell me to leave my brain at the time clock." This perception of not being welcomed in the decision making process lingers and can only be dispelled by leaders that not only welcome, but *require,* employee involvement at all levels.

5: Including Core Employees in the problem solving process is an essential part of the succession planning process.

6: Including employees is an essential part of the mentoring and development process every organization must have to retain Core Employees and Temporary Employees who have the potential to become Core Employees.

After discussing these six items, most leaders see the light (at least the smart ones do!) and agree that inclusion of Core Employees and the upper level Temporary Employees in the problem solving process increases engagement in the work process and improves the company. All leaders need to change their mindset about employees' roles in the problem solving process and view their inclusion as necessary if their company is going to thrive in the Knowledge Economy. They also need to cut the crap about not having enough time to do it!

THE BOTTOM LINE

14

EXPECTATIONS

Sticking to the Standards

"The nicest thing about standards is that there are so many of them to choose from." —Andres Tannenbaum

I'm pretty hard-core about things when it comes to the workplace. My philosophy is simple, but effective: Reward and recognize those employees who exceed expectations (the Core Employees); train and motivate employees who have the potential to meet expectations, and give them the opportunity to do so (the Temporary Employees); and get rid of employees who cannot or will not meet expectations (the Others).

When I advise my clients on how to implement this highly effective approach to improving performance in the workplace, the first obstacle is not the employee at all. It's the fact that management either has not established standards and expectations or is not enforcing them—and sporadic enforcement, which confuses all employees and gives The Other protective cover, is worse than no enforcement! Since having and enforcing good standards and high expectations is essential to maximizing performance, here are a few rules to start the process:

1: Develop high standards and high expectations. Include the Core Employees' input in this process.

2: High expectations begin in the hiring process. Don't hire people who lack the work mindset (think of Nucor, a steel manufacturer, which establishes facilities in rural areas where they hire workers with the "farmer's mentality"—hard work all day, every day—and train them to make steel).

3: During the on boarding process, leave no doubt in the new employee's minds about the need to meet the expectations and standards by clearly explaining what the expectations and standards are.

4: Use words, *and actions,* to communicate standards and expectations to everyone in the workforce.

5: Accept no excuses for behavior that violates the established standards. No way; no how! Allowing occasional unacceptable behavior means, in time, tolerating routinely unacceptable behavior. Every exception allowed weakens the standard and reduces performance.

6: The standards and expectations need to be periodically reviewed to determine if they still make sense for the company. Only if the Core Employees have an issue with a standard should it be adjusted. Never lower the standards to accommodate low performing employees!

7: Enforce the standards by first disciplining and then terminating those who do not meet them. The Core Employees will applaud you; the Temporary Employees will be motivated to become Core Employees (or leave); and The Others will know their turn is coming.

8: Leaders at every level who do not have high expectations for their work team and do not enforce appropriate standards are automatically classified as The Others!

Does your company have high standards and expectations? If yes, does it communicate and enforce them, or does it only give them perfunctory lip service?

THE BOTTOM LINE

15

HIRING

Upgrading the Workforce

"A crisis is a terrible thing to waste." —Paul Romer

The recent recession caused companies to cut staff and operate lean, and most companies will not return to the staffing levels they enjoyed before the economic crisis in the near future. Human Resources Departments aren't even looking for replacement employees until the need for them is extreme and the workforce is pushed to the limit of their ability to get the work out the door. Work teams are, and will remain, shorthanded since "Doing more with less and doing it better" is very good for the bottom line.

Unfortunately, this has caused Front Line Leaders to keep employees who should not be kept. An example of this occurred several months ago during a focus group I facilitated with third shift Front Line Leaders. I asked them to break their work team into three defined groups: Core Employees, Temporary Employees and The Others. After they quickly completed the list, I asked one (a 30-year Core Employee) why he had placed two employees in The Others category. His response: "They only come to work three days a week, when they are supposed to be here five days a week." When I asked why he had not taken disciplinary action against them, he responded because the crew was always shorthanded and overworked and the pressure to complete the work was constant, he was better off having them work three days a week than not at all! OMG!!

I would think lousy economic conditions would make companies more serious about eliminating poor performers. Instead, based on my own observations and a survey conducted by Caliper, a management consulting firm, nearly 70% of employers find it easier to manage "the devil they know" than to take the risks of hiring unknown new people! WOW!! The idea that 70% of companies are "enduring poor performers" is extraordinary! Rather than accept poor performance based on the mindset things could be worse with new employees, companies should view difficult times as an *extraordinary opportunity* to dramatically improve their operations by "trading up"—replacing poor performers with employees who have the capability to become Core Employees.

My recommendations to start the "trading up" workforce improvement process include:

Continually Getting Rid of The Others and the Prima Donnas! Continually evaluate all employees, at every level of the organization, to find and purge the company of The Others, regardless of their seniority or the positions they hold. Also, when a prima donna—an employee who thinks he is irreplaceable—starts to warble by demanding extraordinary treatment, it's time for him to go. This ongoing employee pruning process provides openings for replacement Core Employees.

Start interviewing to find Core Employees NOW! How many Core Employees in your industry are available now? Identify and start interviewing them in preparation for hiring them once The Others are eliminated and positions are available.

Create a Pay-for-Performance system attractive to Core Employees! Wages and benefits comprise approximately 50% of every company's costs. Most companies have developed compensation programs predicated on an employee's tenure with the company. With steadily rising 3% a year wage increases, virtually equal wages for all workers in a grade or job category, there is little regard for performance and no evidence the compensation paid has any connection between performance and achieving the company's goals.

Not a good process if a company is trying to use compensation to improve performance. Here are some ideas about how to create a compensation program that will attract and retain Core Employees:

Compare! Check out compensation levels in your geographic area annually to determine if the company's compensation remains appropriate at all levels so the company can use its compensation program to attract Core Employees. Remember, competition for Core Employees is not limited to the competitors within your particular industry.

Cash Is King! Attracting and retaining Core Employees requires they view the company's compensation system as "fair and equitable." Translation: more pay for greater performance, experience and training.

Differentiate! Give Core Employees at least double whatever increase is given to Temporary Employees. Don't increase compensation at all for The Others.

Reward Individual and Team Performance! Pay-for-performance programs should be based on both individual and team contribution to increased performance.

Explain Company Benefits! Approximately twenty-seven cents of every compensation dollar is spent on benefits. Because the value of benefits is harder to understand than wages, at least twice a year discuss with employees the value of benefits in the overall compensation package.

Develop a Continuous Operational Improvement Program! Challenge employees, on a daily basis, to improve the operation. And reward them for doing so.

Institute a Comprehensive Training Program! Improve employee communication, conflict resolution, teamwork, performance, decision making and problem solving at all levels of the company.

Rather than remain paralyzed by the challenges of the present and fear of an unstable future, companies need to realize the transitional period of the WorkQuake™ of the Knowledge Economy offers an opportunity to improve their competitive position in the marketplace by continually upgrading the quality of their workforce. Those that don't have the foresight to do this now will definitely regret it later.

THE BOTTOM LINE

16

How Your Organization Can Stop Sucking at Hiring!

"I hire people brighter than me and then I get out of their way."
—Lee Iacocca

A magazine article described how a large city symphony orchestra hired its first chair musicians. Audition notices were sent to qualified individuals. Resumes were collected and those musicians who met the initial qualifications were asked to audition. Nothing unusual with the hiring process so far, right? At the audition, it gets more interesting. The musicians were not announced. The hiring committee, sitting in audience seats inside the orchestra hall, did not know who was playing the selection because the musicians played behind a black curtain draped over the stage to conceal their identities! In this way, the musicians were hired purely on their ability to play and not on their appearance or reputation.

This struck me as an appropriate beginning for a revitalization of the workplace hiring process. A long overdue revitalization!

In the Knowledge Economy, organizations can no longer afford to make mistakes when hiring employees. Hiring the right people and getting them in the right position to have the most impact in the workplace, and on the organization, is one of most important tasks for any leader, and it is essential for any organization committed to excellence through continuous operational performance improvement.

To ensure you are getting the most "bang for the buck" out of the hiring process, here are twelve tips to improve the hiring process and put the right people in the right place:

1: Review Where You Are Getting New Hires!

The best new hires come from referrals by your Core Employees. A referral from a Core Employee is a vested referral. Core Employees make sure referrals will not embarrass them by acting like fools when they are hired. If at least 50% of your new hires are not coming directly from your Core Employees, you need to find out why. (Hint: Do you have a reward plan reflecting how important good referrals are to the company?). Another idea: Print business cards with this on the back: "I believe you would like working for our company. If you are looking for a great career opportunity, call me." Hand them out to anyone you meet (i.e., the fast food employee who impresses you with their level of service) who you think has the potential to become one of your company's Core Employees.

2: Keep the Pipeline Full!

Most companies advertise and interview for positions only when there is a vacancy. Wrong! The hiring process should be ongoing and based on the turnover rate and shrinkage of the qualified labor pool. To effectively meet the need for new employees, determine the rate of turnover per job per quarter by examining the last two years of data. Next, analyze how many immediately replaceable employees, or "The Others," you have. Add 10% to this number to cover the unforeseen, and develop a hiring forecast for each quarter for each position. Start interviewing and don't stop until you have a year's worth of replacements! Make your interview process ongoing and geared towards compiling a list of potential employees who will be contacted when needed. Lots of effort? Absolutely! Required effort? Only if you are serious about meeting the ongoing hiring needs for vital positions within the company! And if any position is not a "vital" position, why does it exist? (the exception: the position the owner's wife's brother occupies).

3: Hire for Attitude!

Few jobs in the Knowledge Economy require a very specific skill set. Knowledge Economy jobs require an attitude that accepts and likes continuous operational improvement that requires showing up every day, learning new competencies, staying until the job is complete and being a productive member of the team. Develop the *Ideal Employee Profile*, and you'll see the technical requirements for most jobs rank low on the list of what it takes to be a Core Employee. Use the *Ideal Employee Profile* to hire for attitude, and then train for aptitude!

4: Hire Based on an *Ideal Employee Profile!*

Hire new employees based solely on their potential ability to meet the expectations and requirements of the *Ideal Employee Profile*. An *Ideal Employee Profile* should be established for each position in the company and should contain: 1) a detailed description of the job; 2) the skill set necessary to perform each function of the job; 3) a list of the attributes of the Core Employees who perform the job; and 4) any other items considered essential for an employee to perform the job at the highest level of productivity and efficiency—including communication skills, teamwork ability and attitude. The *Ideal Employee Profile* is realistic and doable because it is based on Core Employees who are already meeting the expectations and standards listed in the *Ideal Employee Profile*. At every quarterly performance improvement session, the new employee's progress towards becoming a Core Employee should be objectively measured based on their closing of the gap between where they were at the last quarterly review and where they need to be.

5: Realize Interviewing is the Absolute Worst Way to Hire an Employee.

People who want a job are very good at convincing those that interview them that they are the right person for the position. While we think we are great judges of character, often we are not! Accordingly, interviews never shed any light on a potential employee's future performance unless they focus on identifying specific skill sets and determine how a candidate applied those skills in the past in specific situations.

6: Use Simulations, Which are Good Predictors of Job Performance.

During the interview process, require candidates to demonstrate they possess the necessary skill set to do the job by placing them in situations they will encounter doing the job and observing how they respond.

7: Do an Initial Employee Assessment to Predict Future Job Performance.

While most companies perform background checks and physicals, few conduct personality and skill assessments of job candidates. By using a pre-hire assessment (such as Myers-Briggs) and a scenario assessment (have the candidate actually perform a task related to the job for which they are being hired), you can determine if the job candidate has the minimum skill set to perform the job and is a cultural fit before you hire him or her. This requires the realization that "one size does not fit all" in job assessments. There needs to be a different assessment for production workers than for sales professionals. Supervisors and trainers can determine through on-the-job training if a new hire is going to be successful, but why waste company resources on placing a new hire into the system if the person isn't a good match to begin with?

8: Stop Letting Human Resources Do the Hiring!

Involve the collective intelligence of the work team as the real opportunity to revamp the hiring process and make it more predictive of success. At the risk of giving every HR Professional and employment lawyer in the U.S. a heart attack (because they believe if anyone else does the hiring, it will result in Equal Employment Opportunity Commission charges and lawsuits), let's accept the fact HR does not do a good job hiring people to work at jobs they know very little about. So, while HR should perform the pro forma hiring tasks (i.e., background checks, physicals), the hiring of a new employee should primarily be handled by Core Employees who will be training and working with the new employee. Since Core Employees realize their future wellbeing is dependent on hiring the right people, they better recognize both potential high-value and low-value personnel during the interviewing process. This increases the odds of hiring future Core Employees—and that The Others will remain unhired! The best way to avoid dealing with The Others is to not let them into the company in the first place! While Core Employees must be trained to participate in the hiring process, including them will increase their job satisfaction and the chances that new employees will be a better fit for the company. Let's label that a win-win for everyone!

After the pre-assessment testing, drug testing, physical and background checks, bring your team into the hiring process by:

a: Allowing them to eliminate all unnecessary work connected to the job and make sure the proper work related processes are in place. Then have the team review and revise the job description and the skill set needed to do the job. Often, job descriptions have become obsolete, and HR continues to hire for a position that exists in theory, but not reality. Only the people actually doing the work know this.

b: After training them as to what it can and cannot legally ask, HR needs to hold the traditional interview—but this time, with the team interjecting their questions about the candidate's ability to do the work. While a candidate may be able to fool the person who doesn't perform the job on a daily basis, they will seldom fool employees, who want this person to carry their share of the workload.

9: Replace the Traditional Trial Period with a Transition Period!

I don't get traditional trial periods. Notice how much harder employees work during their trial period—when they are attempting to qualify for the job? And notice how their performance declines once the fixed trial period ends and they have the job? That's because a traditional trial period—one with a defined beginning and end—generates a specific mindset: *Once I complete the trial period and have the job, I can relax and expend less effort doing the job than I had to expend to get the job.* In the Knowledge Economy, we are all on a perpetual trial period based solely on our ability to show the organization we continue to bring discernible value to the organization. Yet, the traditional ninety-day trial period persists!

Organizations need to say goodbye to the traditional trial period by eliminating this counterproductive mindset and replacing it with a Transition Period. The Transition Period allows the organization to determine if the new employees can do the job and fit into the company's culture. The Transition Period has no defined parameters: it ends when an employee demonstrates, by behavior or performance, he or she should or should not be an employee. During the Transition Period, new employees are informed they should only be *starting* to hit their productive stride at the end of the Transition Period, not relaxing into a groove of mediocre performance. This crucial conversation must occur while the employees are still working hard to get the job, since physics and common sense tells us: *a body in motion will remain in motion*! By ensuring employees know the company's goals and begin to understand what they must do to help achieve those goals through individual and team continuous operational performance improvement, the stage is set for new employees to continue to improve their performance during their entire career with the company.

10: Make a Core Employee the New Hire's Trainer!
New employees not only need to learn the technical aspects of their job but also about the company's culture and how to fit into the culture. During the training period, new employees engage in *modeling behavior*, which occurs when humans move into a different environment and act like those around them so they can more easily fit into that environment. New employees model behavior after the person they are most connected to during their initial exposure to the company: their trainer. The attitude and behavior of the trainer, to a great degree, determines the new employee's attitude and behavior. Once established, attitudes and behaviors are difficult to change. Often one of The Others—an employee who should have been fired yesterday!—is assigned to train a new employee because the Core Employees can't be spared from doing their jobs. Because new employees are connected to The Other during their training, new employees model their behavior after the behavior of The Other—which means they perform at less than their potential,

develop a bad attitude about the company and start looking for a better job somewhere else! Yet we remain puzzled by the fact the new employee, who had so much potential when hired, isn't working out! It's time to realize training new employees is one of the most important jobs in the company and assign Core Employees to do this essential task!

The Core Employee trainer's job is to ensure the new hire is able to do the job and to determine if the new hire has the potential to become a Core Employee. To make this determination, the Core Employee trainer needs to look for these attributes in the new hire:

> **a:** Is the new hire a "fit" for the company's culture? Does he/she have the interpersonal skill set (i.e., communication, conflict resolution, decision making) necessary to perform effectively within the organization's culture and interact appropriately with team members?

> **b:** Does he/she have the ability to improve the organization and the team by their involvement in the work process?

> **c:** Does he/she have the ability to do the job and the attitude to care about the job?

> **d:** Does the new hire have the physical ability to do the job? Some new hires find the job too physically taxing, even if they passed a company required physical.

> **e:** Does the new hire have the mental acuity to do the job? Some new hires can't perform the mental tasks required (e.g., comprehending written and verbal instructions).

If any of these attributes is missing, the organization has not hired an employee who can improve the organization and the hiring decision needs to be revisited.

To make the new hire assessment process more effective, the trainer needs a weekly New Hire Checklist to track the new hire's progress.

At the end of every week, the trainer submits the checklist to the team's leader. If the checklist shows there is an issue with the new hire, the trainer and team leader discuss it. If, at any time, the leader and the trainer agree the new hire is not going to "cut it", they notify HR and the new hire is terminated immediately. If there are no issues, the leader and the trainer submit the weekly assessment to HR. At the end of the training period, the leader and the trainer submit their written recommendation that the new employee should be permanently hired.

A formalized new hire assessment procedure eliminates bad hires and reduces turnover. (Hint: rewarding the trainer when a new employee reaches his or her first anniversary creates even more motivation for trainers to prepare new hires effectively).

11: Don't be Afraid to Pull the Trigger!

At the beginning of my teaching career, I told every class everyone in the class started with an "A", and only through their poor performance would that grade be reduced. I quickly realized I was making a poor assumption, since my expectations for the members of the class had not yet been met and not everyone in the class was capable of doing "A" level work. After that realization, I began telling my students everyone started off with a "D" and needed to show me, through their performance, that they deserved a higher grade by meeting clearly established expectations. I believe this approach establishes expectations and the level of tension necessary to generate higher performance, not only in the classroom, but also in the workplace.

New employees need to know what expectations they must meet and that they must continually improve their performance. If it becomes evident a new employee is not meeting expectations and does not have the capacity to become a Core Employee, then the decision to terminate that employee must be made quickly. Companies can no longer afford to invest time, energy and resources in an employee that everyone realizes is not a good organizational fit. Yet managers are reluctant to pull the trigger if they are vested in the new employee because of their involvement in the hiring process that selected the new employee in the first place ("How will it look if I terminate a person I just recommended be hired? Better to give them some more time and training and hope they get better at performing the job.") How can this "I don't want to accept the blame for a bad hire" syndrome be circumvented? By basing any decision on (a) face-to-face evaluations between the new employee and the new employee's direct report, (b) the Core Employees who recommended the employee be hired and who are working with the new employee on a daily basis, and (c) the new employee's trainer. At the end of each face-to-face evaluation, those involved give their opinion as to whether the new employee should be retained, and the manager then makes the decision. These new hire evaluations should be conducted each week for the first four weeks of employment, every other week for the next two months, monthly for the following three months and then quarterly forever! Yeah, I know you are thinking this is overkill evaluation. And it is—if your company can afford to keep hiring the wrong people!

12: Ask Them Why They Are Leaving.
Conduct an exit interview to discover the reasons why a Core Employee or someone who had the potential to become a Core Employee is voluntarily leaving. If the hiring process is working (employee referrals + Core Employees involved in the hiring process = hiring employees with potential to become Core Employees), then you need to find out why potential Core Employees are not staying. Exit interviews with these employees will reveal weaknesses in employee job satisfaction that need to be eliminated to increase employee retention. By the way, when one of The Others voluntarily leaves, celebrate with everyone on the team by having cake!

A word about hiring a "rock star" from another company: don't!

According to Boris Groysberg in his book *Chasing Stars: The Myth of Talent and Portability of Performance*, a rock star's performance decreases sharply when he or she moves to another organization. It may take them up to five *years* to return to their previous performance level. I absolutely agree with his assessment. While it may look like a high performer is making magic and huge numbers on his or her own, they inevitably are either prima donnas—who hack off everyone else in the organization because they receive preferential treatment—or their performance plummets because they don't have the support system that was in place at the previous organization. Furthermore, your organization's culture, system and employees will not be supportive of the transplanted rock star, regardless of how enamored you are. Better to hire and develop your own rock stars.

Effective hiring is one of the primary components of building an organization that can thrive in the WorkQuake™ of the Knowledge Economy. Either start hiring better or get ready to be run over by a company that is.

LAYOFFS

Be Discriminating When Laying Off Employees

"Small is the number of people who see with their eyes and think with their minds." —Albert Einstein

As bad economic conditions force companies to lay off employees and reduce pay and benefits, the number of charges alleging age, race and sex discrimination filed with the Equal Employment Opportunity Commission continue to increase. While no company can stop an employee from filing a charge alleging their layoff or wage reduction was an act of discrimination, here are some ways to reduce the odds an employee will win such a case:

1: Reduce the workforce only for a legitimate economic justification.

There needs to be a credible economic justification for layoffs. Using an economic downturn to get rid of poor performers is okay. However, immediately hiring their replacements is inviting a charge of discrimination.

2: Map out what the company's workforce will look like after the layoffs have occurred.

Attorneys often attempt to prove a discriminatory practice or disparate impact case using statistics. If the layoffs disproportionately affect a given protected group (e.g., age, sex, race), re-evaluate the decision making process, or prepare to defend the decisions leading to the disproportionate outcome.

3: The layoff criteria.

A layoff criterion provides the guidelines for determining who should be laid off. Employers should develop the criteria used to select employees for layoff before it occurs. Why? The company must present a "legitimate, non-discriminatory business reason" for why it laid off the employee when responding to a charge of discrimination. While objective factors, like those set forth here, are the easiest to defend in a discrimination charge, subjective factors (e.g., attitude or work ethic) also need to be considered when deciding which employee to release. Objective factors to consider are:

a: Performance.

Use past performance appraisals and other records of performance when making a layoff decision. If an employment decision is based on measurable performance issues (e.g., absenteeism and productivity), the employee will have difficulty winning a discrimination claim.

b: Skills.

Which employees perform essential functions for the company and have the knowledge, skills and abilities needed for the company to remain competitive? The answer should guide layoff decisions.

c: Seniority.

Seniority (last hired, first laid off) is not the preferred way to determine which employees to lay off since it might eliminate high-performing or high-potential employees. Seniority should be a consideration only when the decision falls between two employees with comparable performance records, skill sets and attitudes.

While subjective factors are more difficult to defend in charges of discrimination, they are an essential part of developing effective layoff criteria, since a determination as to which employee should be laid off and which should be retained is often based on intangibles like attitude. When you lay off an employee for subjective factors, involve at least two Front Line Leaders with actual knowledge and experience of the individual's work. Then have an oversight committee review individual selections to ensure that legitimate, non-discriminatory reasons are used to select the employees for lay-off.

4: Communicate.

The most common reason employees file charges of discrimination is because of their perception that they were treated unfairly. To dispel this misperception, the company must communicate the justification for the layoff to each affected employee. This communication should be done by someone other than the employee's immediate Front Line Leader to make the layoff process more objective and harder for an employee to claim he or she was laid off by someone who had a bias towards them.

5: Clean house.

To avoid the possibility of charges of discrimination, managers may decide not to include "trouble" employees (The Others) in the layoff. Not a good thing! This is nothing less than workplace blackmail! A layoff is an opportunity to remove marginal employees from the workforce. This is good for the remaining employees because they see you know who is performing and who isn't, and it is good for the organization since there will be fewer of The Others to adversely affect productivity. Remember, after getting rid of one of The Others by any legal means, have cake!

6: And—here comes the "recovering" lawyer in me (once a lawyer always a lawyer even when no longer practicing law!)— always Document! Document! Document!

LAYOFFS

One for All and All for One

"All for one, one for all, that is our device."
—Alexandre Dumas, *The Three Musketeers*

Acco Brands is an office products supplier that, during previous downturns in the economy, laid off employees. During the latest economic downturn, Acco executives decided to cut its two thousand employees' wages by 47% rather than to cut anyone loose. While such a drastic move defies conventional wisdom that layoffs are the best way to immediately reduce labor costs, I applaud Acco for taking a more constructive approach. Rather than lose any more talent, Acco made a play for team unity.

While no company wants to lay off employees or implement pay cuts, when costs must be reduced to ensure the survival of the organization, implementing pay cuts rather than layoffs is the best approach to follow. This approach encourages the attitude of "one for all and all for one" while eradicating the prevailing attitude of "what is in it for me?" While no company wishes for a disaster, when faced with economic struggles, companies have the opportunity to emphasize and support teamwork by reducing wages across the board and not eliminating employees. In the long run, that is definitely better for the organization and the employees.

For you non-believers, let me offer supporting evidence for the controversial concept that reducing wages is better than laying off the organization's talent during difficult economic times:

Evidence that layoffs help improve organizational performance is weak. I can find no studies showing that layoffs improved a company's long-term financial performance. However, studies do show layoffs either had no significant effects on increasing performance or negatively affected those still employed—the survivors.

Layoffs focus too much on immediate savings of labor costs but not enough on the long-term HR costs and negative consequences associated with the layoff. A Bain & Company study—*Debunking Layoff Myths*—found, because of the negative effects of layoffs on the survivors' productivity, it took companies twelve to eighteen months before the financial benefits of a layoff kicked in. By the time the savings from layoffs kick in, the economy and company is probably in recovery mode. The company must then spend the money saved from the layoffs to hire and train new employees to replace those valuable employees who were laid off.

Layoffs destroy the team concept. The current recession has intensified feelings of being part of a team in the workplace. A survey by Towers Perrin found a growing sense of "shared destiny" with employers—76% of respondents stated they were personally motivated to help their company succeed. To capitalize on this trend, companies need to strengthen the team concept by having the entire team share in the sacrifices necessary to make the company successful.

However, if the decision to reduce labor costs is to reduce wages rather than lay off employees, then follow this Pay Reduction Blueprint so the morale of your entire workforce remains strong through this difficult process:

1: Before reducing wages, undertake a selective layoff to eliminate The Others. If the low performing members of the workforce remain employed and there is a pay reduction, morale and performance suffers.

2: Know the amount of financial relief the company needs—
and get that amount. There is only one opportunity to bite into this
apple. Reducing pay a second time is inviting disaster.

3: There needs to be employee buy-in for the pay reduction.
Communicate effectively about the need for the reduction in pay
before it occurs. Include the employees in the process, stressing, "we
are all in this together." Employees want to participate. Let them.

4: A drastic pay cut must be temporary.
Employees need to know that, in the future, there will be an opportunity to recover their economic loss.

5: The monetary sacrifice must save jobs.
After the pay reduction, there can be no layoff of employees, or
employee morale and performance will suffer greatly.

6: Really Share the Pain.
To expect employees to accept a pay reduction and remain high-
performance workers, the pay reduction must include everyone,
from the President/CEO/Owner down. Furthermore, the highest
paid employees need to accept a greater pay percentage reduction
than the Front Line Leaders and employees. Employees know that
a 50% reduction from a $250,000 salary does not hurt nearly as
much as a 50% reduction from a $40,000 salary.

7: There can be no corporate Prima Donnas.
If there are corporate Prima Donnas—managers or executives who
are arrogant, difficult to work with, not team players, manipulative,
privileged, demanding, unreasonable, displaying a high opinion of
themselves not shared by others—they will destroy employee morale and performance.

A company can do more than the seven steps listed in my Pay Reduction
Blueprint. However, they cannot do less and still retain the high level of
employee morale and performance necessary to keep the company successful during times of required shared sacrifice.

THE BOTTOM LINE

19

MISTAKES

If You Mess Up, Fess Up!

"Confession is good for the soul." —Scottish Proverb

"Confession is good for the soul." Doesn't that sound wonderful? Yet, how many of us really believe this soulful concept applies to the workplace? If we confess our mistakes, won't we look weak and incompetent to our boss, employees and customers? Isn't it better to cover up our mistakes or blame them on someone else?

I've got news for you: that tactic doesn't work anymore—if it ever did! Just ask Toyota.

While it's tough to admit making a mistake, leadership quality often depends on the honesty generated by admitting a screw-up. For example, one manager I coached was the classic finger pointer—he never accepted the blame for any mistake, even those clearly his responsibility, and he would always place the blame on someone who worked for him. This irritated his employees to the point they began to carefully document his involvement to ensure they would not be to blame when a HUGE mistake occurred. And a HUGE mistake did occur. Ten thousand dollars of defective inventory was not returned to the manufacturer in time, and the company had to eat the entire amount. When the manager had to explain why this error had occurred, he attempted to place blame for the mistake on another employee who produced e-mails establishing it was the manager who was responsible for the error. The result: when the evidence of the manager's attempt to avoid responsibility for his mistake became apparent, he lost his job.

A similar situation occurred when another manager's mistake caused a truckload of product to not ship on time, causing the company to lose a good customer. In this instance, because he did not attempt to cover up his accountability for the mistake, the manager was not fired.

Learning how to accept responsibility and accountability is essential to being a good leader and maintaining the support of the workforce.

Still need convincing? Here are the primary reasons you need to Fess Up When You Mess Up:

1: Everybody already knows you messed up.

Who do you think you're kidding when you attempt to cover up your mistake or blame someone else for your error? In the Information Age, everyone has access to the information necessary to determine who is responsible for the screw-up. And someone will find and reveal that information.

2: You are sending a message that erodes respect and trust.

Do you really want your employees and boss to assess your character and leadership abilities based on your attempt to avoid accountability or perpetuate a cover-up (otherwise known as "lying")? What do your actions say to customers about what constitutes acceptable behavior in your organization?

3: It's the cover-up that gets you.

Martha Stewart didn't commit the actual crime of insider trading, but she went to prison because she attempted to cover up her unethical activities by lying to a federal official—a definite no-no. Her refusal to admit her unethical behavior and her attempt to cover it up cost her five months of incarceration in a federal prison camp. What will a failure to fess up cost you?

4: There is economic value in admitting a mistake.

When doctors apologize directly to patients for the harm they cause, malpractice claims are reduced by more than 50%. While I don't know what positive economic impact admitting your mistakes could have on your relationship with your customers and employees, I do believe not doing so will definitely create a detrimental economic impact through lost sales and employee turnover.

Everyone makes mistakes. How we deal with those mistakes is what matters most and is one of the defining acts of leadership—good and bad.

THE BOTTOM LINE

20

MOTIVATION

Has Extrinsic Motivation Left the Building?

"I don't motivate my players. You cannot motivate someone. All you can do is provide a motivating environment and the players will motivate themselves."

—Phil Jackson, L.A. Lakers coach

I have always been a big P4P—pay for performance—guy. Rewarding employees for every increase in performance seemed to be the way to go. Now, not so much. The latest recession swept away the remaining vestiges of the Industrial Economy's Command and Control style of management (yeah, I know Command and Control has made a comeback—as dictatorial practices always do in times of great fear, but believe me, it's only temporary). Now, it is becoming more apparent that the way we compensate for performance is archaic: paying employees an hourly wage to perform tasks only causes employees to take more time to perform the task or requires more supervision to ensure they do not milk the clock since more time spent doing the job, not caring about the job, equals more money.

Using extrinsic motivation—raises, bonuses, time off, etc.—to attempt to increase performance has some value in workplaces where rote or routine tasks can't be avoided (e.g., assembly line work). However, at best, extrinsic motivation generates only short-term results because of the ever-escalating sense of entitlement it encourages: *employees will perform at the lowest level for which they are rewarded.* Can you seriously blame them since they are selling their labor by the minute?

Consider Vasili Alexeyev, the super heavyweight Soviet Olympic weight-lifter of the 1960s and 1970s. The Russian government rewarded him with a pre-determined amount of money each time he broke a world record—which he did, many times. In fact, he broke the world record at every weightlifting event in which he competed—by exactly one-quarter of a pound! He had no incentive to perform at his highest level to collect the extrinsic reward!

Like Alexeyev, 80% of employees who are not Core Employees perform only at the level necessary to collect an extrinsic reward. Once they have collected the reward, they may stop performing or even sacrifice other aspects of the work (e.g., quality).

The traditional application of extrinsic motivation is a tired idea in to-day's workplace where organizations need their employees to be self-directed high performers. Yet, the use of extrinsic motivation won't die easily because most leaders continue to subscribe to Theory X assumptions about employees (nearly all employees suck and need to be forced to work) and believe the employees' only interest in the job is money; therefore, employees will show little ambition to perform at a higher level without an incentive based motivation program.

However, there is an alternative. Instead of using extrinsic motivation to attempt to generate high performance, successful leaders are using an integrative motivation strategy that emphasizes performance and satisfaction equally, based on these elements of *intrinsic motivation*:

1: Giving employees more control over their jobs.
This does not mean giving up control over what employees are re-quired to do, but rather over the methods employees use to accom-plish what they are required to do.

2: Giving employees the opportunity for development.
Helping employees develop the skill set necessary to do the job, presenting them with challenging work that keeps the job interesting

and then developing them so they can move into a more demanding job within the organization.

3: Recognizing employees need a defined purpose (hopefully, aligned with the organization's strategic goals) that allows them to not only do the job but to also *care* about the job.

As Bob Dylan sang, "The times, they are a changin'." For an organization to thrive in the WorkQuake™, the way greater employee involvement, commitment and performance is generated needs to reflect the changes occurring in the Knowledge Economy.

THE BOTTOM LINE

21

PARTNERS

The Power of Partners vs. Pawns

"In the past a leader was a boss. Today's leaders must be partners with their people. They no longer can lead solely based on positional power." —Ken Blanchard

Have you ever thought about your employees becoming your business partners? If not, you had better start! The only way leaders can engage the people who work for them after the onslaught of the latest economic downturn—downsizing, furloughs, pay reductions and lack of appreciation—is to stop treating people like employees and start developing the Partnership Relationship!

In the WorkQuake™ of the Knowledge Economy, the concept of employing a person as an employee is an outdated holdover from the Command and Control Industrial Era. The Partnership Relationship is the only relationship that will ultimately allow a company to be successful. Why? Because partners *not only do the work, they also care about the work!* That is the game-changer in a nutshell.

If leaders want to unleash the untapped potential of employees by turning them into real partners and not just associates, then they should read the *Power of 2* by Rodd Wagner and Gale Muller. I consider this required reading for any leader who expects his or her organization to be successful while moving forward in the WorkQuake™ of the Knowledge

Economy. *Power of 2* outlines how to create a Partnership Relationship with employees by following these eight elements:

1: Complementary Strengths.
Everyone has weaknesses—even (gasp!) leaders! Employees have strengths that can complement a leader's weaknesses. Leaders need to acknowledge their weaknesses and then compensate for those weaknesses with the strengths of work partners.

2: Common Mission.
Establish the same agenda for everyone in the organization. By aligning everyone with the same goal, it will be achieved.

3: Fairness.
No one receives the short end of the stick if the partnership is to succeed. When the good results are shared fairly, everyone accepts the sacrifices necessary to achieve the common goals.

4: Trust.
Partnerships succeed only when the partners trust each other to get the job done and have each other's back.

5: Acceptance.
Accepting and celebrating the fact each partner brings a different skill set to the partnership is key to a successful partnership.

6: Forgiveness.
Partners make mistakes. Failure to forgive those mistakes equals a failed partnership.

7: Communicating.
No one is a mind reader! Constant and meaningful communication is necessary to prevent misunderstandings and to generate an efficient work process between partners.

8: Unselfishness.
When partners become as concerned with seeing their partners succeed as they are with their own success, the partnership will be successful.

Wagner and Muller also highlight the potential inherent in a Partnership Relationship with the company's employees:

1: Teams headed by a partner, and not a boss, engage twice the number of employee partners.

2: Partners deliver a higher level of performance than employees, who are traditionally not trusted and are either bribed with pay increases (the carrot) or coerced by threats of layoff and reductions in pay (the stick) so they will work harder.

3: Engaged partners deliver a higher level of performance than employees. They have:

- 27% less absenteeism

- 30% less turnover

- 62% fewer accidents

- 12% better customer service

- 18% higher productivity

- 12% higher profitability

Based on this information, it is apparent that organizational success in the WorkQuake™ of the Knowledge Economy is dependent on changing the leader's mindset from "I'm in charge" to "We're in charge." So, go welcome your new business partners already!

PERFORMANCE

10 Tips Guaranteed to Improve Organizational Performance

"Don't lower your expectations to meet your performance. Raise your level of performance to meet your expectations. Expect the best of yourself, and then do what is necessary to make it a reality." —Ralph Marston

Since everyone is interested in improving performance at every level of the organization, and organizational and personal improvements are my forte, here are Ten Tips Guaranteed to Improve Organizational Performance:

1: Communicate the Company's Goals to the Workforce.

95% of the company's employees have no idea what the company's goals are. Aligning employees' efforts with organizational goals is essential for successful performance improvement.

2: Stoke the Competitive Spirit.

Develop a competition between your company and another company in an area the other company does very well and in which your organization needs to improve. And the other company doesn't need to know there is a competition!

3: Conduct Survey and Focus Groups.
No, you do not know what your employees are thinking.

4: Do a Compensation Survey.
Know what the marketplace is paying, and compete for and retain your talent by paying at least that level of compensation.

5: Develop an Effective Pay-for-Performance Plan.
Skip the annual pay raise and instead reward employees for meeting established work objectives.

6: Develop an Effective Recognition/Rewards Program.
Recognition and Rewards Programs that are customized, individualized and varied motivate employees to improve performance.

7: Practice Financial Education.
Most employees think your company keeps fifty cents of every dollar of revenue! Share financial information so employees know how much it costs to run the business.

8: Improve Employee Performance Improvement Sessions.
Conduct quarterly employee performance improvement sessions based on the Ideal Employee Profile.

9: Train Your Front Line Leaders.
Provide training so Front Line Leaders will respect employees and interact with them more effectively and more frequently.

10: Walk Around More.
The more visible you are and the more you ask, "How are we doing?," the more performance increases.

You were expecting more? Sorry, but there is no secret formula for increasing employee performance. It's all hard work, but organizations that are serious about it achieve spectacular results.

Crank Up the Competitive Spirit!

"A competitive world offers two possibilities. You can lose. Or, if you want to win, you can change." —Lester Thurow

As a part of the performance coaching program I initiated among a client's nineteen Regional Managers, we developed a $5 million challenge to ensure the company was profitable in the last quarter of the year. Each of the nineteen regions needed to generate their portion of the $5 million over a sixteen-week period. Each region's weekly sales results were posted so every employee in the company could see the weekly results. Each regional manager developed an Action Plan to achieve the region's goal by including every employee in its development. By including the employees in developing the Action Plan needed to meet this challenge and by posting each region's results weekly, the competitive spirit was generated among the employees in each region, which resulted in the employees generating the sales necessary to reach the $5 million goal. Because of the revenue generated during a traditionally slow time of the year, anticipated layoffs were prevented.

In my experience, properly framed indirect internal competition, with employee input and buy-in and a clearly communicated achievable goal, will generate unexpected positive results. Why? Because employees love competition! One way to channel that competitive spirit into Continuous Operational Performance Improvement is by developing a company-wide "Beat the Competition Program." Here's how to set up this program:

Select the Competition: Identify a specific area of the company that needs to be significantly improved to increase productivity and profitability (i.e., customer service). Select an industry leader in these specific areas. Make that company the competition.

Set a Specific Time Frame for the Competition: Set specific company-wide goals to meet to beat the industry leader (e.g., improving on time delivery to customers or improving the safety record). In a company-wide meeting, announce the details of the competition and the meaningful prize (Don't be cheap! A meaningful prize makes this process really hum.).

Make each Employee Group a "Team" and the Leaders "Facilitators and Coaches": Each coach will act as a facilitator to a team and assist the team in deciding how they can improve operational processes and do their part to beat the competition. The team develops and submits their written game plan for implementing operational improvements to management. Every week, the team meets with their coach to review the progress made towards reaching their team goals and submits a weekly progress report to management. What gets measured will get done!

Hold Monthly Meetings: Once a month, company leaders meet with each team to review and reward their progress and to discuss how the competition is going.

Celebration: When the competition is over, and the specific company-wide goals to beat the industry leader are met, the entire company celebrates the victory!

Repeat: Now do it again! Only better!

Cranking up the employees' competitive spirit can produce significant performance improvements and increased productivity. And it can be a helluva lot of fun!

PERFORMANCE REVIEWS

Annual Employee Performance Reviews Blow!

"Performance is your reality. Forget everything else."
—Harold Geneen

A frequent question from my clients is, "Isn't an annual review of an employee's performance enough to improve that employee's performance?"

My Answer: NO! Why? Because annual employee performance reviews are a waste of time and effort! What conceivable reason could any Workplace Leader have for allowing an employee's poor performance to go unaddressed for twelve months before doing anything to improve it? Especially when many employees perform at 50% or less of their potential! Companies are quick to take action when an employee's behavior is so bad it requires discipline or discharge. However, that is only the tip of the employee improvement process that should be addressed on a timelier basis.

By addressing employee performance issues informally on a daily basis and formally on a quarterly basis, Workplace Leaders can effectively and objectively review performance based on the Ideal Employee Profile, and the goals agreed to by the employee and set forth in the employee's

Individual Performance Action Plan. Quarterly performance improvement reviews not only show employees the organization and their Workplace Leaders care about their performance, but also eliminates the need to discipline most of them. Because of this regularly received attention, employees immediately become more productive since employees will focus on what their immediate Workplace Leader pays attention to. Shocking? Not so much, because the relationship between an employee and their direct report is the most important managerial relationship an employee has within the organization.

Since annual employee performance reviews seldom generate the desired outcome—a more productive, motivated employee—think about them only as one piece of the productivity improvement process (and not a very good piece at that).

POSITIVE THINKING

The Power of Positivity

"A positive attitude may not solve all your problems, but it will annoy enough people to make it worth the effort."
—Herm Albright

The attitude of people in positions of responsibility has a greater impact on employee performance than most managers or supervisors realize, especially when employees feel vulnerable to layoffs, wage reductions and changes in working conditions. Because employees collect 80% of their information from the non-verbal cues Front Line Leaders give, and not from the words they speak, the actions of Front Line Leaders really matter to employees who determine how things are going throughout the workday, and within the organization, by observing how Front Line Leaders are acting at any given moment. For that reason, I always remind the Front Line Leaders—managers and supervisors—that because they are in positions of responsibility and authority, they are under constant scrutiny by everyone in their work group or department every day and in every way. If Front Line Leaders constantly wear worried expressions, everyone in the workplace is adversely affected! If everyone in the workplace is affected, so is overall workplace performance.

I'm not suggesting Front Line Leaders act like Little Miss Mary Sunshine, and I'm definitely not suggesting being untruthful with the workforce. If the company is struggling to survive, the employees have a right to know that information. But if the message is, "we're not out of the woods yet but we're working on it," it is important for Front Line Leaders to display "positivity"—the state of being positive.

Barbara Fredrickson, a researcher at the University of North Carolina, supports my position that managers and supervisors have the ability to influence the workplace and make it more productive by being positive. In her book *Positivity,* her research shows managers with greater positivity are more accurate in making decisions and more effective in their relationships with employees, and they infect their work groups with greater positivity, producing better coordination among team members and reducing the effort needed to get work done. In addition, research shows that work teams with a positivity ratio of 6:1 (for every negative statement or interaction, there are six positive ones) are high performance, while teams with a positivity ratio of 1:1 are low performance. Manager or supervisor positivity begins to have an impact on improving employees' performance *at a 3:1 positivity ratio* (3 instances of positive actions to 1 instance of negativity).

While positivity doesn't keep bad things from happening, because Front Line Leaders are on "stage" from the moment they enter the company's parking lot until they leave, how they choose to react to hardship—either positively or negatively—influences how others in the workplace react. The company's success may very well hinge on the amount of positivity Front Line Leaders bring to the workplace.

Don't know if you are being positive enough? Then check out your positivity level and find out how to increase it at www.positivityratio.com.

THE BOTTOM LINE

RECOGNITION

Hey! Look at me!

*"There are two things people want more than sex and money...
recognition and praise."* —Mary Kay Ash

The company's employee recognition program (your company does have one, right?) sends an important message about the company's priorities and value. It reinforces and rewards the actions and behaviors the company wants to see from its workforce, and it invites employees to perform at a higher level. An effective employee recognition program is simple and immediate, and it reinforces desired employee behaviors/ actions if the program characteristics include:

Aligning Employee Behaviors and Actions with the Company's Goals. Recognition must be directed at specific employee behaviors and actions that achieve the company's clearly communicated expectations and goals.

Everybody Participates. Any employee who acts or behaves in accordance with the recognition program criteria must receive recognition—even one of The Others! This requires developing recognition criteria with specific information about what behaviors and actions will be recognized.

Fairness. To avoid even the hint of favoritism, the employees, not management, should select which employees will receive recognition.

Visibility. Employees must be periodically (e.g., quarterly) reminded about the recognition program.

Consistency. Management must consistently and constantly recognize specified employee actions and behaviors.

Differentiation. An effective recognition program builds upon what each employee wants and creates the action steps to earn it with specified behaviors that benefit the company.

Timeliness. Effective recognition occurs as soon as possible after the desired behaviors or actions occur, reinforcing and causing the desired behavior to continue.

Variety. Effective recognition programs must be changed periodically (e.g., semi-annually) to provide an element of surprise and to ensure it does not become an entitlement.

An effective recognition program doesn't have to be expensive to be effective. But it does require constant attention, creativity and, just maybe, a little fun.

Now Is the Time to Be Fast and Furious!

"If everything seems under control, you're just not going fast enough." —Mario Andretti

Faced with the economic devastation caused by the recession and potential bankruptcy, a company retained me to assist them with the restructuring of their organization. After the first meeting with the six-member management team and a review of the company's finances, it was apparent the company would not survive another six months if it continued to hemorrhage money on non-productive operations and un-productive personnel. Within six weeks, the management team and I had conducted an in-depth review of the finances and twelve-month prospects for each of the company's five separate operations and determined two of them did not have viable futures. Those two operations were shut down within seventy-two hours after the review was completed. This "fast and furious" approach—quickly reducing operational expenses—generated the cash flow necessary to stop the downward financial spiral and gave the company the time needed to develop a comprehensive restructuring plan. By developing a "fast and furious" approach, twelve months later the company is profitable, in a growth mode, and seeking an acquisition to capture additional market share.

Business leaders constantly pose the question to me: during a crisis, can a leader actually be too fast and too furious? My answer is an unequivocal,

"No!!" I believe this proactive approach to a crisis is required from every company that wants to succeed in the post-recession economy. Here is why I strongly recommend you be fast and furious:

The Worst Is Over: There is no reason for a company's leaders to still have the deer-in-the-headlights look. At this point, the company has taken the worst the recession has to give and remains standing. The necessary layoffs, pay cuts and cost-cutting measures have been implemented. Now it is time for companies to give themselves a pat on the back for surviving and plan for their success in the post-recession economy. That means changing the organizational mindset. How?

Stop Hoping the "Good Old Days" Will Return: The "good old days" are gone, never to return. Speeded up by the sudden restructuring of the economy, the transition from the Industrial Economy mindset to the reality of the Knowledge Economy—the WorkQuake™—has moved into its last stage. This does not mean there won't be good days, but it does mean they won't come as easily as they did pre-recession. It's a waste of time and energy to continue to pine for the "good old days." Focus on success in the new reality of the Knowledge Economy. Companies must start living in the world as it is by...

Seizing the Day: Now is the time to get ready to rock and roll! Companies that were poorly managed or overleveraged are disappearing from the marketplace. This presents unprecedented opportunities to increase the customer base and grab market share—if the company is preparing now for the economic recovery by setting...

"Big Hairy Audacious Goals" (to borrow Jim Collins' phrase). Now is the time to examine and, if necessary, revise or change every aspect of the organization's operation. This includes hiring practices (so the company never again hires one of The Others), compensation (develop an incentive based pay system), performance improvement (change from managing to coaching) and process improvements (by letting the person doing the job improve the job process). Now is the time to instill the mantra of *Doing More With*

Less and Doing It Better in every manager, supervisor and employee because...

A Time of Change = A Time for Change: Fear, as long as it is not mind numbing, generates great energy necessary for organizational innovation and change. Because of the fear created by the current economic devastation, everyone, even employees who normally are resistant to changes, are not only aware the old ways don't work anymore, but are also willing to consider doing things differently. This is the absolute best time to institute organizational change.

You can never be too fast or too furious when faced with a challenge like preparing for the post-recession future and the reality of the Knowledge Economy. Remember, fortune continues to favor the bold!

RESTRUCTURING

Tips for Knowledge Economy Employers

"It don't come easy. You know it don't come easy." —Ringo Starr

Now that you have a term—the WorkQuake™—for that uneasy feeling you have that there is no stability in the workplace or the marketplace (and all this time you thought you were imagining it!), you can consider what you need to do to not only survive, but also thrive in the WorkQuake™ of the Knowledge Economy.

And here are Nine Thriving Tips for Knowledge Economy Employers:

1: The Knowledge Economy Formula for Success: ½ X 2 X 3 = P(2).

Half the Workforce (get rid of the The Others, who comprise 20% of the workforce, and the 30% of Temporary Employees who do not have the capability to become Core Employees), when Paid *Twice* As Much, will produce *Three Times* As Much, equaling Greater Profit and Productivity (P2) (formula courtesy of Charles Handy). Don't think your company can do this and survive? You are 100% wrong!

2: It's the Core Employees.

In the hyper-competitive environment of the Knowledge Economy (rapidly expanding technologies, global competition, higher customer expectations), every company must distinguish itself in the marketplace based on service and productivity. A company's Core Employees provide the essential service and productivity differential.

3: Hire Core and Temporary Employees, but Retain Only Core Employees.

Core Employees are the indispensable talent to your business because they have the skills and attitude necessary to make your company a high performance organization. Temporary Employees have the potential to become Core Employees. Temporary Employees who do not become Core Employees become The Others.

4: Eliminate The Others Now.

The Others are the Employees who should have been fired yesterday. My question to you: Why is even one of The Others still employed?

5: Keep Your Core and Temporary Employees Happy by Continually Upgrading Their Skill Sets.

Give them every opportunity to learn new skills and competencies that will make them more flexible company resources.

6: Reward Them.

Align performance pay with the company's goals. Reward Core and Temporary Employees with performance pay when they use their skills to help the company achieve its stated goals. Give The Others nothing!

7: Recognize Them.

Double, triple, and even quadruple the number of "atta boys" and "atta girls" for effort beyond expectations by Core and Temporary Employees. Research establishes high performance and employee engagement are based on five instances of positive recognition for every occurrence of negativism in the workplace. Your employees are keeping count even if you aren't.

8: Engage Core Employees.

Make Core Employees an integral part of the organization by asking their opinions, implementing their ideas and giving them more control over their work.

9: Prepare for the Next Economic Boom-Bust Cycle.

The WorkQuake™ of the Knowledge Economy makes the workplace inherently unstable for the foreseeable future. Prepare for it and learn to live with it.

Now stop only surviving and start thriving!

RESTRUCTURING

What's the Plan, Stan?

"If you don't know where you are going, you will wind up somewhere else." —Yogi Berra

A Strategic Plan is the basic roadmap that describes, in clear and simple terms, how the business will travel from where it is to where it wants or needs to go.

In uncertain times, every company needs a one-year Strategic Plan that points to future certainty and calms the nerves of everyone in the organization. In addition to a master Strategic Plan, every department or team within the company also needs a one-page departmental Strategic Plan—developed by the employees in that department or on that team—that aligns what the department does on a daily basis with what the company wants to achieve overall.

Why emphasize this type of strategic planning?

The business terrain has changed, so last year's Strategic Plan cannot and does not reflect the new roadmap the company needs to follow.

Employees need to know a company-wide Strategic Plan is in place. A Strategic Plan emphasizes that management is in charge, has a plan that fosters confidence in the future, and knows how to steer the company to where it needs to be.

Involving the employees in developing departmental Strategic Plans ensures they understand the company's overall Strategic Plan and how they can contribute and help the company achieve the Plan by their daily activities in the workplace. This involvement generates the employee commitment every company needs to thrive in the Knowledge Economy.

The existing uncertainty about the future also provides the perfect opportunity for the company to focus the strategic planning process on the changes needed at all levels of the organization to ensure the company's future. This is because strategic planning creates movement in three stages:

1: The Unfreezing Stage (overcoming resistance to change);

2: The Moving Stage (accepting change); and

3: Refreezing Stage (making the new change part of the organization).

Recent economic challenges have dramatically reduced the opposition to change reflected in the Unfreezing and Moving stages and have created a unique opportunity to develop and implement organizational changes (Refreezing) to reflect the needs of the organization, its employees and customers.

Unfortunately, most Strategic Plans are only 50% effective in achieving their goals because:

Employees don't understand the Strategic Plan and their role in it. Ninety-five percent of employees don't know what their company's Strategic Plan is and don't understand how their work relates to the Plan's success. Employees with knowledge of the company's strategy, who see a clear connection (or "line of sight") between what they do and how they can contribute to the success of the company, have heightened levels of commitment, job satisfaction and trust. Without the buy-in of the company's most important stakeholders—the employees—who must be relied on to implement important elements of the Strategic Plan, the company cannot realize its full potential.

Employees are not involved in developing the Strategic Plan. Since the strategic planning process is usually created only at the top level of management, other employees—those who have to implement the Plan—are not involved in the planning process. It is the height of hubris to assume that only top management has answers to issues (especially internal issues) that will determine the fate of the company over the next twelve months. Since there is no question that engaged employees give their company crucial competitive advantages (i.e., higher productivity, lower turnover and revenue growth), doesn't it make sense to engage the employees in one of the most important tools for the company's success?

The current economic crisis presents the ideal opportunity to improve the potential for the success of the Strategic Plan by:

- Rejecting the idea employees are not capable of strategic planning.

- Explaining the company's Strategic Plan for the next twelve months and the barriers the company faces in implementing the Strategic Plan.

- Requiring every department or team to develop a one-page Strategic Plan, establishing its alignment with the overall Strategic Plan, and a one-page Action Plan detailing what will be done to ensure the success of the Strategic Plan.

- Once a quarter, meet with each work group to discuss how the Action Plan should be adjusted.

At the end of twelve months, celebrate the success of the Strategic Plan.

In a time of ongoing crisis, it is imperative that every company that wants to thrive in the Knowledge Economy enlists the cooperation of its employees in order to succeed. The involvement of employees in the development of the one-year Strategic Plan generates the engagement, alignment and commitment needed for organizational success in the time of the WorkQuake™.

So, what's your company's plan, Stan?

THE BOTTOM LINE

30

No Guts = No Glory!

"Fear of failure must never be a reason not to try something."
—Fredrick Smith

After conducting a workshop on Continuous Operational Performance Improvement, the company's president and I engaged in a rigorous debate over my recommendation his company implement the following formula for success in the WorkQuake™: $\frac{1}{2} \times 2 \times 3 = P(2)$. As described in The Bottom Line #3, this formula (courtesy of Charles Handy) simply means that Half the Workforce, when Paid Twice As Much, will produce Three Times As Much, equaling Greater Profit and Productivity (P2). The president responded that his company was already a "lean, mean fighting machine" and it would be impossible to operate if half the current workforce was eliminated. He also dismissed the second part of the formula because if half the workforce was eliminated, paying the remaining half of the workforce twice as much as their current salaries made no sense since the marketplace allows the company to hire and retain "good" workers at the company's current rates of pay.

My response to his arguments:

On a daily basis, 50% of a company's employees are only doing enough to not get fired! Moreover, 80% of employees could perform significantly better if they wanted to. Don't believe me? Then ask your company's Front Line Leaders and discover what I continually assert: the company's Core Employees are working at

100% of their potential; the Temporary Employees are working at between 50 and 80% of their potential; and The Others are working at less than 50% of their potential. Since fear can be a great temporary motivator, these numbers may be skewed during bad economic times because even The Others can be momentarily scared into performing better—but their improved performance will not last. Based on this information, do the math and you'll see that getting rid of half the workforce that is not working to full potential is not an extreme idea. Eliminating The Others and the low-performing Temporary Employees will please the Core Employees, who hate carrying the non-performers, and will cause the remaining Temporary Employees to work harder at becoming Core Employees.

No Company should be hiring and retaining only "good" employees! Companies need to hire and retain "great" (not "good") employees. The only way to recruit people capable of becoming Core Employees is to utilize a hiring process that identifies high performance potential and offers starting wages significantly greater than the competition. To develop, retain and motivate Core Employees also requires greater levels of compensation. Cash is still king for most employees. While the annual 3% wage increase does not motivate them (anything less than a 10% increase has no motivational value), they would be motivated by a 100% increase, especially if that level of compensation was predicated upon performance that had to produce significantly greater profits.

The constantly changing marketplace of the WorkQuake™ of the Knowledge Economy demands Companies continually re-evaluate business processes and increase the value of their human capital if they are going to thrive. Winners and losers are determined by the ability to shift perspective and do things differently. The burning question: Does your company have the guts to do things the way they must be done to achieve success in the WorkQuake™?

THE BOTTOM LINE

31

RISK

Risky Business?

*"It's not because things are difficult that we dare not venture.
It's because we dare not venture that they are difficult."*
—Iroquois Chief Seneca

One of my favorite stories about a desperate person taking a desperate chance and succeeding is about Fred Smith, CEO of FedEx. In 1973, Smith did not have enough money to make the company payroll. He flew to Las Vegas, played blackjack, won $27,000.00 and was able to pay the employees. The rest, as they say, is history.

Even though Smith's story is an extreme example of risk taking, it highlights the fact that risk is a fundamental part of business. While I'm not advocating you bet the farm (or the company) on a roll of the dice in Vegas, I am suggesting you must always take reasonable risks in your business. While others are hunkering down with that deer-in-the-headlights look, waiting for the "right time" (the right time is always now!) or hoping things will return to "normal" (which ain't going to happen), you should assess your operation, company and industry to determine where the opportunities for growth and value lie. There are always opportunities—especially in bad economic times! While a robust and growing economy will support nearly all companies, good and bad, a retrenching economy has no tolerance for a poorly run company. That means the opportunity for the acquisitions of available material, equipment, people and entire companies at a fraction of what they would cost during "good times" abound.

Still, many leaders are reluctant to take a risk because they fail to recognize the difference between rewarded and unrewarded risk. Here is the distinction:

Rewarded Risk is about potential opportunities that can create value for the company. While Rewarded Risk probably has some downside (it is still risk, after all), the potential upside is clearly, and objectively, much greater than the potential downside.

Unrewarded Risk is all downside. Unrewarded Risk provides little, if any, objective opportunity to create increased value for the organization. It's taken either out of sheer desperation or to feed a leader's huge ego. In either event, it destroys existing value.

Once a leader understands the difference between Rewarded and Unrewarded Risks, there is no excuse for not taking Rewarded Risk. In fact, researchers at the University of British Columbia found that the organizations headed by leaders who took greater risks are more successful. However, only one-third of all leaders will take even Rewarded Risks! The other two-thirds are either too timid and miss out on opportunities to improve their operation and increase value for the company, or are reckless or desperate (e.g., Fred Smith) and take Unrewarded Risks that damage the company. (It should be noted that Fred Smith focused on Rewarded Risks after his trip to the blackjack table, as FedEx's growth over the last thirty-five years bears out).

To become a successful risk taker, managers need to develop and practice these risk taking traits:

- Be a realist—an optimist with reasonable reservations—in assessing an opportunity for success or failure.

- Be confident in the ability to deal with potential consequences.

- Allow for the possibility of losses, but don't be overwhelmed by them and do not allow them to alter the decision making process.

- Be able to continue to see the Vision—the end results—even in the midst of the inevitable crisis of confidence.

- Have enough experience to be able to rely on intuition—the ability to come to the right conclusion when you haven't been given enough information.

The measure of good risk taking is whether the value of the company increases as a consequence of taking the risk. When was the last time you took a Rewarded Risk or encouraged someone else to do so?

RULES

Seriously, What's Up With All the Rules?

"Ninety percent of what we call management consists of making it difficult for people to get things done."
—Peter Drucker

I hate rules! Most of them are an overreaction to the continuous disruptive behavior of 20% of employees (The Others) that generates a collective punishment for the entire workforce. The more rules in a company, the more likely the company suffers from a serious infestation of The Others in the workforce. Rules de-motivate the 80% of the workforce who would seldom, if ever, violate them by telling them "we really don't trust you to do the right thing". More frustratingly, The Others are the best workplace "lawyers." They know all the company's rules and how to abuse them, while adroitly avoiding the consequences of their actions. For example, The Others will constantly accumulate twenty-nine points under an attendance policy where thirty points will get them suspended. And they know the exact day on which they will drop enough points to be able to take another day off and still not get suspended! Finally, most rules irritate Core Employees who occasionally face situations where the rules created to deal with The Others are imposed upon them indiscriminately. And why would a company ever want to irritate its Core Employees?

Rules are also reminiscent of the Industrial Age since they represent the insecurity of management and its ongoing futile attempts to assert control over the workplace. Of course, this type of control can only be accomplished by reducing the methods employees use to get the job done properly. This approach restricts the high level of performance every organization wants from their employees by restraining productivity and innovation. Often, Core Employees are required to ignore company rules in order to get the work done most efficiently. Hardly the way to develop the caring versus doing attitude needed from the workforce to thrive in the Knowledge Economy! Yet, management continues to pile on the rules for everything from how to dress to how to act in the workplace.

How ridiculous can rules become? Take this example, not from a private company, but from an elected governmental body where free speech is allowed and needs to be encouraged. The Finance Committee in the Village of Elmhurst, Illinois, removed a resident from an open meeting because she rolled her eyes and sighed when one of the committee members was speaking on a proposition to which the resident was opposed! Of course, I assume, if the resident had worn a sidearm to the meeting and had not rolled her eyes and sighed, everything would have been a-ok!

Unfortunately, the workplace is no better. A German company is terminating employees who complain more than three times about the working environment! Perhaps instead of penalizing the complainers through a new rule, management should resolve the issues about which they are complaining. Just a thought that, if verbalized, could get me labeled a complainer by this employer.

In my experience, organizations not functioning well in the Knowledge Economy have lots of rules but very unclear expectations. To foster a productive workplace and continuous operational performance improvements, there needs to be as few rules as possible and very clear and achievable expectations. What's the difference between rules and expectations? Rules are constraints that inhibit the ability of Core Employees to care about the work while giving The Others the cover they need to only do the job. "Working to Rule" (only doing what is absolutely necessary to escape punishment) is the way The Others ensure they can't be punished for not doing enough since they have met the requirements of the rule (e.g., producing so many pieces per hour). Expectations outline the parameters of performance but don't restrict exceeding those parameters.

To address the issue of too many rules, I recommend a once a year "Get Rid of the Stupid Rules Day!" Accept the fact everyone in the company knows the rules of the workplace, and then purge the system of all rules that govern behavior. I know that any HR professional reading this will want to hunt me down and hurt me, but the reality is that companies cannot continue to treat employees like prisoners. Rather than continue to be rule-obsessed based on the false belief that rules are going to resolve your people problems, get rid of the people who *are* the problems and give the other 80% of employees the autonomy to do their jobs in the most productive and efficient manner possible—and don't encumber them with useless rules! Treat employees like the partners they should be, and see what the reality of the Knowledge Economy Workplace looks like!

Seriously, you do not need all those rules!

$\underset{\text{THE}}{}$ BOTTOM LINE

33

SURVEYS AND FOCUS GROUPS

The Value of Free Night in the Workplace

"If there is any one secret of success, it lies in the ability to get the other person's point of view and see things from his angle, as well as from your own." —Henry Ford

Raising two boys—redheads yet!—provided many opportunities for me to discover how to better communicate about the important things in their lives. When the boys were eight and nine, it occurred to me—based on my own experience growing up and being deceptive with my parents—that maybe they were not being forthcoming about what they were doing when their parents weren't around.

To counteract this lack of crucial information, "Free Night" was created. Free Night occurred once a month, when the boys, my wife and I sat down after dinner and discussed what was going on in our lives. Nothing unusual so far, right? The "unusual" occurred when we told the boys that on Free Night it did not matter what they revealed to us, there would be no consequences! Now I, being as delusional as most parents, hoped my boys would be open and honest about whatever mischief they were getting into. At some point, though, they had decided there were things we were better off not knowing because of how we would react—and the consequences that knowledge could potentially have for them! Free Night presented them with the opportunity to share with us the cool—and questionable—stuff they were involved in, and nothing would happen. Since everyone wants to share, Free Night intrigued them.

However, they were understandably suspicious. In the past, there had been consequences when they were involved in questionable behavior (like the time they shot the pizza delivery guy's car with a pellet gun, and I arranged for them to spend an hour in jail). Knowing there would be some disbelief about the no-consequences aspect of Free Night, we overcame it by sharing the questionable behavior we engaged in as kids their age to establish "common ground." They were amazed and delighted that we revealed this entertaining information!

After two Free Nights, where we shared and encouraged them to do likewise, they opened up and told us what they were really doing when we weren't around. Fortunately, none of it rose to the felony level or jeopardized the personal safety of themselves or others, but some of it was still hard to hear and not become openly upset.

Free Night was a gradual process, with a lot of testing on their part to make sure we weren't going to get mad or rat out their friends. It took a lot of restraint not to react negatively while still giving them constructive advice and observations, but it provided valuable information about what was going on in their lives that we never would have received otherwise. It also gave us the opportunity to change our parenting skills. There were never any consequences, and we never ratted out any of their friends—even though we did nudge them away from certain kids.

Free Night ended when the boys began actively dating and I had become bald from too many Free Nights! But it was a great concept while it lasted. Now, I not only recommend it to parents but also to managers—but only if they really want to know the truth.

How does the Free Night concept operate in the workplace? While managers hope their employees are sharing important information about what is transpiring in the workplace, the reality is they are not going to hear very much. Employees have learned there are usually unfavorable consequences for revealing the truth about managers and the effects their management skills are having on performance, productivity and profitability. So, employees keep their opinions to themselves. Even when asked, they seldom reveal more than a glimpse of the truth.

While this is not the way to run a healthy business, it is the reality of most workplaces and will remain the reality until management starts establishing common ground, inviting the truth, and is willing to hear and handle the truth without reacting adversely.

There are two ways to gain the benefits of Free Night: employee satisfaction surveys and focus groups. Both methods will yield valuable information if their purpose is clearly understood and properly administered, and the information collected is utilized to institute positive changes in the workplace. A few simple rules of the road to get you started:

1: Employee satisfaction surveys and focus groups should be conducted by an independent third party with a guarantee of anonymity. Employees have been burned too many times to believe management is an impartial third party when it comes to hearing the truth about the workplace.

2: The survey should be administered on company time and participants paid for their participation so the greatest response is generated.

3: Focus groups are always better than surveys. Follow up a survey with focus groups that gather specific information from Core Employees about the issues highlighted by the survey.

4: Within thirty days, do something positive with the collected information. If you ask for information and then do nothing with it, morale will grow worse. And good luck obtaining accurate information in the future.

5: Do a six-month follow-up to determine the effectiveness of the response to the issues raised.

Finally, if management can't handle the truth, don't ask for it.

SURVEYS AND FOCUS GROUPS

Can You Handle the Truth?

"You can't handle the truth!"
—Col. Nathan Jessup, A Few Good Men

Remember the scene in *A Few Good Men* where Col. Nathan Jessup, played by Jack Nicholson, says under cross-examination, "You can't handle the truth!"

Let me paraphrase that question: Can your company handle the truth?

Not long ago, a "simple" day surgery turned into three days in the hospital and a painful recovery period. While trapped in my hospital bed, watching inane daytime television and frequently hitting the morphine button, the hospital took the opportunity to use the TV for a customer satisfaction survey. This led me to think about why more companies don't recognize the value of employee satisfaction surveys and focus groups.

I'm a big believer in the value of surveys and focus groups, but most of my clients are not. The more progressive among them do annual customer satisfaction surveys, using outside firms to ensure they collect the right information. They evaluate that information and make changes to improve their relationship with customers. These companies recognize that by including the customer as a stakeholder and asking for input about how to make the relationship better, they ensure ongoing loyalty at a time when loyalty in the marketplace is hard to find. Yet, these same companies fail to see the value in an annual employee survey or periodic focus groups that allow the employees—important stakeholders in the company—to express their opinions about how their relationship with the company can be improved!

As I reflected from my hospital bed, I believe most companies think the annual employee survey or focus group is a waste of time and resources for the following reasons:

Companies think their employees will let them know about problems in the workplace without being asked. Wrong! Most employees are not willing to openly criticize their managers in the best of times unless invited to do so *and* promised protection from retaliation. In times of company distress, an open dialogue between employees and management is even less likely to occur, since employees who would offer constructive advice do not want to be seen as "complainers" who are unaligned with the company's goals.

The company's leaders think they know how employees will respond to survey questions. Leaders who are not on the front line every day receive filtered information—and the farther removed from the front line they are, the more filtered the information they receive. Properly structured employee surveys and focus groups remove those filters and reveal, with surprising accuracy, the organizational barriers restricting increased employee engagement and impeding improved employee performance.

Leaders don't want to be held accountable for the poor performance of their work group. Surveys and focus groups establish accountability for performance. Properly constructed surveys provide a measurable "snapshot in time" for each work group, which identifies specific work issues linked directly and objectively to employee performance. Once these issues are identified, measurements can be created and implemented and accountability for future performance placed with the appropriate group of employees and their leaders.

Management doesn't care about what employees have to say. Command and Control managers don't want to hear that they should be doing a better job. There will be no improvement in employee performance until management realizes they aren't doing the best job.

Leaders are afraid they will have to take action. Once issues are revealed by a survey or focus groups, the expectation is that leaders will constructively deal with those issues to improve the company. Failure to enact those improvements will further decrease employee performance and engagement.

Employees in every organization have something important to say about how to make the company better. Companies truly interested in Continuous Operational Performance Improvement must listen to their employees through periodic surveys, focus groups and individual conversations with Core Employees.

Team = Together Everyone Achieves More

"When a team outgrows individual performance and learns team confidence, excellence becomes a reality."
—Joe Paterno

A **definition of teamwork is:** the ability to marshal individual relationships and talents into a whole whose output exceeds the sum of its parts.

In the Knowledge Economy, work is most effectively completed through high performance work teams because:

1: High performance work teams make both the job and company better.

Work groups get the job done. Work teams get the job done better.

2: High performance teams work *on* the work, not just in the work!

They focus on continuously improving performance. Team members constantly question the way things are done in the work process. This creates a high level of employee engagement and generates operational improvements.

3: High performance teams provide these advantages:

a: They produce more ideas and information than individuals do.

b: They produce higher quality decisions and solutions.

c: They improve understanding and acceptance among team members.

d: They have higher motivation and performance levels.

e: They are more likely to generate innovation.

Since I conduct organizational team-building workshops throughout the country, I think about the ever-changing reality of teams in the workplace. While everyone in management gives lip service to the importance of building a great team, the reality is most of those in charge really don't want a team; they want a high performance *work group*. The difference? Members of a work group do exactly as they are told and nothing more, while members of a team *receive the authority and responsibility to do whatever is necessary to get the job done right and improve the work process.* Work groups are limited in how much value they can add to the organization, while teams can elevate the organization to the next level because they develop Core Employees, whose collective output vastly exceeds the sum of any individual.

There are three barriers every organization faces when transitioning from work groups to teams:

1: Giving Up Control.
Most managers and supervisors are afraid to give up control to the employees who actually do the work because they fear they will become (or be seen as) useless.

2: Trusting Employees.
Most managers and supervisors continue to exhibit Command and Control tendencies when it comes to how they relate to employees and how they do the job.

3: Patience is Required.

High performance teams don't develop overnight. Team members must be trained in how to function at this high level and how to avoid and overcome the conflicts inherent in teamwork.

A year ago, I began assisting a company president who had read my paper on the effect of the WorkQuake™ on the workplace. He decided that if the company was going to make it to the next level, its workforce needed to make the transition from a command and control management style, where work was accomplished by traditional work groups led by supervisors, to self-directed work teams. As with most change initiatives, the supervisors in charge of the work groups staunchly supported the status quo (if the work groups became self-directed work teams, what would they do). So did certain employees (can we all say The Others?) who realized that increased responsibility would carry with it increased accountability. The Others definitely wanted none of that!

To overcome the inherent resistance embodied in the status quo, I involved all employees in the change initiative by holding focus groups. I explained the reason why the change to self-directed work teams was necessary; making sure everyone understood why this would be beneficial not only for the company, but also for the employees. The increased savings and increased profit based on increased productivity generated by the work team would be shared with the work groups that successfully transitioned to work teams. No one—including supervisors—would be adversely affected by the change.

Team members also need to accept responsibility for the performance of everyone on their team. For this to happen, team members must first understand it is their job to maintain the necessary level of performance to get the job done. Then the team must be given the authority to act and receive training in how to use its authority to improve overall team performance. Without the necessary buy-in, authority and training, team members will complain about an underperforming member, but no one will take the action necessary to improve performance. The "it's not my job" syndrome will kick in.

I created a ninety-day training program in team communication, decision making and conflict management to transition the work groups to work teams. This program also developed the supervisors into coaches and facilitators who would assist the work teams. Of course, none of this works—especially the buy in—if the team realizes management is only paying lip service to the concept and is still making the decisions. Management needs to convince team members of its commitment by requiring them to fashion their solution to legitimate performance issues, including those concerning team members (i.e., failure to perform at an acceptable level after being given adequate training, resources and an opportunity to improve). While the facilitator or coach can guide the team in resolving this issue, he or she can't tell the team what to do.

I selected one work group, already at a high level of performance and made them the test group. When they successfully made the transition to work team, they received public acclaim before the entire company and a cash bonus. Members of the new work team were designated as trainers to help the other work groups make the same transition. They also assisted me in tweaking the transition process and training program so they became more effective. This approach requires the team members take their obligation to be responsible for team productivity seriously. One way to highlight this obligation is to base a certain level of compensation on the overall performance of the team. Once each team member has something to gain or lose tied directly to team performance, he or she will begin to take responsibility for the actions of all team members.

At the end of one year, after having received quarterly counseling, the 20% of the supervisors and employees who remained adamant in their opposition to the work team concept, and could not function effectively in that environment, were terminated.

The self-directed work team concept remains the most conducive structure to developing high performance in the Knowledge Economy. However, as this example illustrates, it is not an exercise for the faint of heart or the impatient. Every organization seeking to thrive in the Work-Quake™ of the Knowledge Economy must embrace and implement the self-directed team concept in the workplace—now!

The Sink or Swim Attitude

"The only risk of failure is promotion." —Scott Adams

I sat in a coaching session with a regional manager who was conducting performance reviews for his twenty-one branch managers. He told me four of his branch managers, all very good front line employees before being promoted to managerial positions, were not meeting expectations and in danger of losing their jobs. I asked him if he was providing ongoing performance development to address their performance deficiencies. After a long pause, the manager admitted he thought they didn't need any additional development. His reason: They were promoted from within the organization and should know how to do the job. I responded that was apparently not true, because they weren't meeting his performance expectations!

This coaching conversation highlights the sink-or-swim attitude leaders often adopt when it comes to employees. After all, if employees didn't already have the necessary skills to do the job, why would they be promoted in the first place? What leaders don't realize is, in most instances, an employee promoted into a new position has been thrown into the deep end of the pool and left to sink or swim on his or her own.

Most internal promotions are based on a leader's determination that a front line employee, who is doing a great job in their current position, can be successfully promoted to a higher-level job as a supervisor or manager. While the new job requires a different skill set, the leader assumes the great front line employees either already have the necessary skill set or should be able to figure out what he or she has to do to succeed in the new position on their own.

This assumption is not necessarily true. Unfortunately, leaders often have blind spots when it comes to understanding a Front Line Leader's development needs. They think if they play well in the shallow end of the pool as Core Employees, they will automatically be able to swim as supervisors or managers when they haven't been taught how to manage. This is a BIG mistake to make! An employee's ability to do a good job in their current position is seldom a good indicator of ability to perform well in another position, especially one requiring he or she possess and use a different set of required skills. And those different skills are seldom organizational (those required to do the job), but most often are interpersonal (those required to get other employee to do the job). Research supports my position:

1: A 2010 report from Bersin & Associates reveals that "HR leaders rate their first-line managers as their 'least ready' work group, even less capable than their entry-level employees." WOW!

2: Only 57% of Front Line Leaders said they possessed the skills they needed when they first stepped into their managerial position.

3: The most common undeveloped skill set reported relates to core interpersonal managerial skills—communicating, decision making and delegating.

4: Less than 30% of new managers have a development plan aimed at getting or improving the required managerial skill set for their new position.

5: Less than 60% of new managers believe the company is committed to their development!

Clearly, most Front Line Leaders are being promoted into managerial positions without having the required skill set to actually manage. Definitely not the way to maintain or improve organizational performance!

Better insight into a Front Line Leader's readiness to become a manager is required so The Gap between actual skills possessed and the skills required to perform the duties of the new job can be addressed and eliminated. These developmental needs can be determined through a variety of means, including personality, behavioral and 360-degree assessments. Once a newly appointed manager's areas of strengths and weaknesses are determined, a development plan with clearly stated expectations can be created. Then an Action Plan with specific action steps and time line can be developed to ensure the new manager actually completes the development plan. Accountability must be a part of any Action Plan, not only for the newly promoted manager, but also for the manager's boss, because the success of this process is predicated on the new manager receiving the needed support and guidance from their manager. Organizations must do a better job of providing their new managers with the skills needed to thrive in their new positions, or it won't only be the new managers who are facing a sink-or-swim alternative.

VIRTUAL MANAGING

Virtual Managing & Virtual Coaching

"There are managers so preoccupied with their e-mail messages that they never look up from their screens to see what's happening in the non-digital world." —Mihaly Csikszentmihalyi

Virtual management, because you are working almost exclusively with people off-site, requires a different style of managing. But while the virtual world is rapidly tearing down old traditions, certain managerial techniques continue to be effective, whether employees are onsite or off-site. To maintain an effective virtual team, virtual managers still need to:

1: Provide inclusive leadership that supports, rather than controls, the team.

2: Clarify team members' roles, responsibilities and accountability.

3: Articulate a vision for the team.

4: Get good results from the team by being accessible and staying well connected to team members.

5: Coach and develop team members.

6: Bring together necessary resources so the team can get the job done.

7: Be decisive when required.

8: Be honest with team members.

9: Respect each team member's expertise.

10: Give appropriate feedback based on data and observation.

11: Do not engage in favoritism.

12: Provide technical training so the team can do its job.

13: Provide interpersonal training so the team members can work more effectively with their managers and teammates.

As you can see from the list, the requirements for being a good virtual manager are no different from those for an onsite manager. However, mastering interpersonal relationships, building trust and coaching are more difficult from a distance. Just as some employees should not be members of a virtual team, some managers should not be virtual managers. Recognize those on your team who are or can become good virtual managers—and those who do their best work face-to-face—and choose wisely by not trying to force a square peg into a round hole.

VIRTUAL MANAGER

Becoming the Virtual Manager

"Executives owe it to the organization and to their fellow workers not to tolerate nonperforming individuals in important jobs." —Peter Drucker

The WorkQuake™ of the Knowledge Economy requires a different way of working. The Command and Control management model followed by most organizations is unsustainable in the Knowledge Economy because the travel required is expensive and consumes managers' time and energy. Now is the time for virtual management—the ability, using technology, to maintain close relationships and manage many people at many locations without the need for face-to-face management and extensive control. Virtual management not only reduces travel cost and wear and tear on managers, but it also generates better team morale and productivity when properly conducted.

The primary challenge of a virtual manager is to build a cohesive team when team members are separated by time and space and the manager can't hear, see or speak face-to-face with those they are leading. To overcome this challenge, virtual managers must:

1: Realize they can't control from afar. They must teach virtual team members to manage themselves—to become the ultimate self-directed work team.

2: Use face-to-face meetings, videoconferencing, chat, e-mail and conference calls to build the team's social structure. By helping team members get to know each other on a personal level, the team can exchange ideas, get feedback, share learning experiences and get different perspectives that will improve trust and the quality of team interaction.

3: Establish operational guidelines clearly defining what the team and its members can and can't do and what each team member's role and responsibilities are.

4: Act as a facilitator and not a dictator to assist the team in overcoming internal barriers and connecting with the outsiders needed for the team to achieve its goals.

5: Select self-starters who can collaborate and understand and value teamwork.

6: Have the right technology in place, and provide appropriate technological training to team members.

Virtual teams that successfully bridge the distance gap enjoy a clear competitive advantage in the marketplace, since they are better able to effectively leverage resources, including time and energy, as they respond to specific challenges and opportunities. Today's technology and business requirements both allow and demand virtual management. It can be done well or poorly. Your call.

THE MORNING
MANTRA

THE MORNING MANTRA

01

ACTION PLANS

The Action Plan Path to Success

"Have a bias toward action – let's see something happen now. You can break that big plan into small steps and take the first step right away." —Indira Gandhi

One of the most frequently asked question by managers is: "Why haven't I accomplished my goals for this quarter?" My most frequent answer: "Because you aren't effectively using your time—not because you don't have enough time."

Executives and business owners I coach often whine, "If I only had another 10 hours a week, I could accomplish my goals." However, the issue is never really about not having enough time; it's what they do with their time that matters. Why? Because time is *finite*—there is only so much of it—and tasks are *infinite*—there will always be more tasks to do than available time in which to do them. So, what really matters is not trying to squeeze another hour out of your work day, but rather examining how to use time to better achieve your work goals.

A BIG part of this examination—and the ultimate way to improve Personal Productivity—is establishing an Action Plan to achieve stated goals. Effective people operate with formal Action Plans, regardless of whether the project lasts a day or a year, because the best ideas have no value until they are actually implemented. Here are the steps to follow to develop an effective Action Plan:

1: Determine Your Attitude: Do you really want to achieve your goals?

2: Make every important goal a SMART Goal:

Specific – Be precise about your goal.

Measurable – How are you measuring progress towards the goal?

Achievable – Is the goal realistic?

Results oriented – Tie a reward to achieving the goal.

Time sensitive – A specific timeframe eliminates procrastination and perfectionism.

3: Develop a written Action Plan to achieve each goal:

a: Sequence every action necessary to achieve the goal.

b: Break each goal down into specific tasks.

c: Place each task into the Action Plan with a realistic date of completion.

4: Maintain daily focus on achieving the specific task by the designated date.

5: Publicize the goal to others—the more the better!

6: Be accountable to someone on a weekly basis for achieving the tasks set forth in the Action Plan.

Most Action Plans are not effective because they don't answer the following questions:

1: Is an Action Plan even needed?
Is this project worth doing at all? If not, don't waste your time! Move on to a more worthwhile project.

2: Is the Action Plan realistic?
Unrealistic Action Plans demoralize those who struggle with the futility of impossible implementation. And make any future Action Plan suspect.

3: Can the clear results of the Action Plan be seen from the beginning?
If not, clarify the purpose of the Action Plan before going any farther.

4: Is everyone who will implement the Action Plan involved in its creation?
Get expressed buy-in. If you leave one required person out of the creation of the Action Plan, you form a barrier to its implementation. Why do that?

5: Are there firm start and end dates?
Set an unequivocal start date to overcome inertia, and an end date to avoid perfectionism.

6: What are the potential "bottlenecks" that will slow the Action Plan down?
Bottlenecks—needed time, resources or people—are inherent in any Action Plan. Bottlenecks inhibit Action Steps and must be recognized and addressed during the Action Plan's creation phase.

7: Is the Action Plan broken down into measurable "chunks," milestones assigned to specific dates?
The more complex the Action Plan, the more it needs to be broken down into "mini-Action Plans." Even a daylong Action Plan needs to be "chunked" into 90-minute segments to be most effective. A year-long Action Plan should be broken down into weekly or monthly

chunks, depending on its complexity and the number of people involved in its implementation.

8: What are the specific, concrete Action Steps for each day/week/month?

Lack of clarity kills Action Plans. Create as many specific Action Steps as possible and plug them into the Action Plan.

9: Have the Action Steps, with a specific completion date, been assigned to those responsible for completing them?

Action Plans are linear in nature. They require Action Steps to be accomplished in a specific order. If the person assigned an Action Step does not complete their task, then the next Action Step cannot be completed.

10: Is there established accountability?

Accountability must be assigned along with Action Steps. The consequences of failing to be accountable must be clearly understood.

11: Is there a Follow-Up Plan?

Ongoing follow-up is essential to ensuring the Action Plan is on track and on pace. A reasonable follow-up plan—short of micro managing but definitely keeping an eye on results—is based on compliance with the action steps.

12: Has the Action Plan been turned into a visual and given to everyone involved?

Make it big and bright, and something to hang on the wall.

13: Is the Action Plan being regularly updated?

Everyone involved likes to see progress. Update the Action Plan on an appropriate schedule—daily/weekly/monthly—and send it to everyone involved.

14: Is enough buzz about the Action Plan being generated?

Keep everyone geeked up about a long-term Action Plan—two weeks or more—with achievement celebrations as milestones are reached.

15: Is the unexpected expected?

Collective flexibility and improvisation—the ability to solve the unexpected—is required to meet inevitable obstacles to the completion of the Action Plan.

16: Is the need for persistence recognized?

The longer and more complex the Action Plan, the more energy is required to complete it. At some point, the energy level will be low, and plain old persistence is required to push the Action Plan forward.

Properly planned and implemented Action Plans delineate the difference between high and low achievers. As always, you get to make the choice. Choose wisely.

$\underline{\overline{\text{THE}}}$ MORNING
$\overline{\text{MANTRA}}$

02

Why Do We Need an Action Plan?

"Man Plans and God Laughs." —Yiddish proverb

Arecent study by IBM made me laugh. It posits that CEOs believe the most important leadership quality for success in business is creativity! At least we no longer have to wonder why most businesses are floundering in the WorkQuake™ of the Knowledge Economy! When will businesses get it right? There is no lack of creativity or ideas for innovation in the workplace. Want to know how to "discover" creativity and innovation that really matters to the bottom line Mr. & Mrs. CEO? Then ask the people actually doing the work for their ideas about how to make processes, products and services better—that's what creativity should be about!

But regardless of where an idea is born, what good is an idea without an Action Plan to turn it into reality? *The best ideas have no value until their implementation.*

The ability to execute, rather than generate, new ideas matters most in the workplace. I am sick to death of hearing executives say, "I'm the idea person." That means they can't be bothered getting their hands dirty with the real work of the idea's implementation. The reality is 50% of their ideas are too impractical to ever be implemented! Yet they drive everyone else crazy with their insistence that time, energy and resources be expended pursuing their impractical idea!

The leader who really matters in the Knowledge Economy can recognize a doable and beneficial idea and then can generate a realistic Action Plan and force the organization to stick to it until it results in the implementation of those creative and innovative ideas swirling all around us. How important is an Action Plan for bottom line implementation results? As calculated by the American Society of Training & Development, the odds of an idea actually being implemented are:

- 10% – hearing an idea you like

- 25% – deciding to implement the idea

- 40% – deciding when to implement the idea

- 50% – planning how you are going to do it

An effective Action Plan also does the following:

1: It requires knowing specifically what problem is being solved and what results are being sought.

2: It requires identification of "The Gap"—the distance between the status quo and the identified goal.

3: It sets forth specific written action steps identifying what needs to be done to close "The Gap" and when they will be done. The more specific the action steps, the more likely "The Gap" will be closed.

4: It identifies the resources and training needed to achieve the results, while forcing an answer to the question, "Is what we are doing really worth the expenditure of time, energy and resources?"

5: It overcomes inertia by creating a bias for action.

6: It creates "Big Mo" (momentum).

7: It sets deadlines and milestones for each action item, providing clarity of purpose, intensity and a needed sense of urgency.

8: It controls the optimism gene that causes 54% of humanity to underestimate how long a job will take and how much it will cost.

9: It forces focus on required tasks and prevents focus on "could do" or "want to do" items.

10: It requires doing the next most important thing.

11: It creates accountability for everyone involved.

12: It causes the realization that there are no "perfect" answers and mistakes will be made, but that "decide and do" beats "think and plan."

13: It creates a willingness to improvise as required by circumstances that cannot be controlled. The required results should not change, but the way you arrive at those results should remain open to constant change.

Implementing an Action Plan is the real difference between high and low achieving leaders. Stop thinking and start implementing!

$\underset{\text{THE}}{\text{MORNING}}$ MANTRA

THE MORNING MANTRA

03

ASSOCIATION

Those We Associate With Dictate Who We Become!

"A man only learns in two ways, one by reading, and the other by association with smarter people." —Will Rogers

I recently read two interesting articles. One stated an individual's net worth is determined by the average net worth of the five people (outside of family) with whom a person spends the most time. The second discussed research reported in The New England Journal of Medicine that people with fat friends become fat. Researchers found those people with a friend who became obese increased their own odds of gaining weight by 57%. On the positive side, the research also found the chances of a person losing weight increase if a friend loses weight.

These two articles illustrate the importance our association with others plays in our lives. Individuals in two Personal Productivity Workshops I conducted commented on how important it is that everyone in their work group, including the leaders, were participating in the workshop. This makes absolute sense, considering how difficult it is to change our daily routine, whether it is what we eat or how we work. Most people realize they need to become better at managing their time, especially after a workshop on Personal Productivity where the tools for improved time management are discussed. But the willpower necessary to actually turn a bad habit into a good habit dissipates as people return to their daily routines.

This is where the importance of group support comes into play. The success or failure of changing one's routine, of turning bad Personal Productivity habits into good habits, depends, to a large extent, on whether the majority of the work group, especially the leaders, accept the principles of improved Personal Productivity and provide the support necessary to allow members of the work group to implement Personal Productivity techniques. This means being supportive and not getting upset when someone doesn't immediately respond to an e-mail or lets a phone call go to voicemail instead of answering it on the second ring. Or better yet, become their Accountability Buddy and actively help them succeed. Who knows? They might just return the favor.

This form of support, associating with people who are trying to achieve goals similar to yours, is extremely beneficial when it comes to changing bad habits to good habits, so don't try to go it alone. Remember, even The Lone Ranger had Tonto.

THE MORNING MANTRA

04

BABY STEPS

Taking Baby Steps is Okay!

"An idea that is developed and put into action is more important than an idea that exists only as an idea." —Buddha

During a Personal Productivity Workshop I conducted for Wheatley & Timmons, a premier public relations firm in Chicago, I realized I was asking the group, comprised of very bright people who are very good at what they do, to do too much too fast. They were skeptical about whether I really could understand their Personal Productivity issues. After all, I have never walked a mile in their PR shoes, so how could I possibly know how demanding their customers are, how difficult every project is or how critical each deadline can be? How could I possibly offer workable techniques to solve their unique set of Personal Productivity issues?

My answer to that very legitimate question: while I do appreciate the differences in businesses, I have found, after 30 years of being a consultant and coach, that, while products and services vary, people do not. The same Personal Productivity issues (e.g., interruptions, scheduling, planning) afflict people who work in manufacturing the same way they do people who work in public relations. However, to dispel the belief my suggestions and techniques may work elsewhere, but not at their company, it is necessary for people to see that when they implement the Personal Productivity tools I suggest, their work and life will become easier and more productive.

Based on my experience at Wheatley & Timmons, let me suggest a new approach for your Personal Productivity program: review the Personal Productivity tools I set forth in this book and then (drum roll please!) throw out the ones you don't like (and, yes, I know the time management audit—keeping track of your activities for a seven-day period—will be the first to go). Take the one suggestion you think is the best Personal Productivity idea for you and implement it within the next 24 hours. For example, I suggested the crew at Wheatley & Timmons not answer their phones or e-mails for a two-hour period. I could tell, by the universal look of panic, that even though it was a good suggestion, it would not be implemented because it was too radical. I immediately regrouped and recommended they try not answering their phones or emails for 30 minutes. Based on the collective relief on their faces, it was an idea they might implement (interesting how, if you want people to try something they find distasteful, if you start them at the extreme and guide them to the not-so-extreme, they might give it a shot!)

The object of this story: baby steps are absolutely okay. After all, the object of all of this stuff is for you to do something to improve your Personal Productivity skills now—and even a *little* improvement will generate a HUGE ROI for you.

THE MORNING MANTRA

05

COMMUNICATION

It's All About... the People

"The single biggest problem in communication is the illusion that it has taken place." —George Bernard Shaw

We often think of managing time as it relates to tasks—the things on our To Do List we must accomplish within a defined timeframe. What we often leave off our To Do List is time to spend with the company's most valuable resource (wait for it!): People.

Setting aside time to talk with the people in your organization fosters a closer, more productive team and prevents employee problems. Good leaders make it a priority to establish solid working relationships with each employee by regularly scheduling one-on-one meetings with them. Nothing says you care more about employees than the amount of time you spend with them. When was the last time you had a conversation with an employee for reasons other than to criticize or give an order? Regularly scheduling fifteen-minute "one-on-one" conversations with each of your employees or direct reports to talk about whatever he or she wants to discuss, builds interpersonal relationships and creates a more positive and productive work environment.

Because you are more open to hearing what they have to say, employees will reveal important things in these conversations they would not normally bring up during the workday. Of course, this requires you actively listen by having a dialogue, not a monologue, with the employee, ensure there are no interruptions during these one-on-one meetings and don't turn the conversation into a performance review!

Also, take some time during the one-on-one meeting to learn what is important to each employee—what makes him or her feel valued and appreciated and what causes him or her stress. Find out how each employee likes to operate, while sharing your own operating philosophies. This is a chance to explore mutual expectations and improve the tone of your working relationship.

By investing in this one-on-one time with your people, you generate a huge ROI as you create Core Employees and employee engagement.

THE MORNING MANTRA

06

DEADLINES

Make Deadlines Your Friends

"Without a deadline, baby, I wouldn't do nothing."
—Duke Ellington

As a one-man band, I have to plan each day for maximum efficiency and profitability, and when I get ready to take a vacation, I become even more focused on what I need to do so my time away will not disrupt my business. And I become more focused than usual on The Deadline— the day I am leaving town. Because I mentally acknowledge The Deadline, I also become exceptionally productive during the days before I leave. I'm willing to bet it's that way for most people.

Here are a few reasons why a meaningful deadline (one we take seriously) cranks our Personal Productivity up a bit:

Focus: A "drop dead date" forces us to focus our attention and energy on getting the required tasks completed.

Excitement: Even though we hate the tension associated with a deadline, there is still a certain amount of excitement generated as we move inexorably towards the end date.

Urgency: Deadlines create a sense of urgency that is often critical to accomplishing goals since we are running out of "messing about" time.

Action: A deadline causes us to act, whether we are ready to or not. The excuses for inaction evaporate as we face the inevitable, and we give it our best shot—then we are done.

While I realize it can be debilitating to face a deadline that is impossible to meet—usually imposed by somebody else trying to manage our time and productivity—there is something to be said for imposing urgent deadlines on ourselves for important projects. This may mean approaching each day as if you were going on vacation tomorrow.

07

DELEGATION

Learning the Delegation Dance

"Surround yourself with the best people you can find, delegate authority, and don't interfere." —Ronald Reagan

An essential part of effective Personal Productivity is delegation—determining what you should really be doing with your time and letting someone else do some of the tasks you are performing. Delegation is about sharing responsibility (the obligation to perform the activities necessary to achieve the required results), authority (the right to act and make decisions), and holding others accountable for their performance (answering for actions and decisions and giving rewards and consequences), while making sure a necessary task is done right by someone else.

One of the toughest things for most leaders to do—including me—is to delegate a meaningful job to another person (do any of us really have any problem giving a job we define as "crappy" to another person to do?). This reluctance to delegate is not only a restrictor on the ability to increase Personal Productivity, but is also an indicator of a HUGE ego ("Nobody can do the job as well as I can!") or a control freak ("They won't do it my way and that is just not acceptable!") or both. It seldom has anything to do with another person's ability to do the job. Because of the impact delegation can have on increasing Personal Productivity (a potential 10% increase), it is a vital skill for any leader to develop because it is essential to have the additional time to get done what needs to be done and, at the same time, to develop others (delegation sounds like a twofer to me!). So, while reining in my HUGE ego and delegating a job to a teammate, I reflected on the following delegation issues:

1: Should Anyone Be Doing This Stuff?

There is no reason to consider delegating a task that no one should be doing! To make a realistic and accurate assessment about delegation, the first thing to consider is whether you or anyone else should continue doing some of the things you are doing every day. Once we settle into our "essential routine," we seldom re-examine the work habits that allow us to complete basic daily routine tasks without reinventing the wheel or thinking about how we should be doing them. Rarely do we consider if we, or a delegate, should continue doing them at all. A scene from the 2002 movie, *About Schmidt*, starring Jack Nicholson, highlights the importance of doing an annual examination of these routine or mindless tasks. After thirty years as an insurance claims adjustor, Schmidt is retiring. His successor visits him in his office, and Schmidt points out an entire wall of bankers' boxes containing the records Schmidt has produced while performing his job. Schmidt tells his successor how important these records are and how invaluable they will be to the successor. A few minutes later, Schmidt is exiting the parking lot as a retiree and sees his successor emptying all of the boxes into a dumpster! If there are "Schmidt" type tasks on your To Do Lists, eliminate them—don't delegate them!

2: What Should Be Delegated?

After eliminating the "Schmidt" type activities, here is how to decide which of the remaining tasks can be delegated to others:

a: Delegate as much as possible so you have more time to do things that are more important.

b: Delegate tasks you are good at because it is easier to train others to do them. An ongoing objection to delegation is that it takes time to train someone to do a task. Nevertheless, consider:

once another person is trained to do the task, you never have to spend your time doing it again. What a great ROI on the time spent training another person to do the task! Furthermore, the person you train will feel valued.

c: Delegate tasks to others who are better at doing those tasks. Hate to tell you, but there are some things you really suck at doing—get over it.

d: Never delegate motivating, teambuilding, praising or reprimanding.

Delegation is difficult because it is primarily a matter of trust (will the person to whom you delegate have the ability and/or desire to do the task correctly?) and control (can you handle the loss of control over the task?) issues. There has to be sufficient trust in the person, or the delegation will not work. That means analyzing each task to decide if it can be delegated and then knowing the delegate has the ability to do the job. Don't delegate to set a person up for failure just to show you're the only one who can do the job (the ego operates in the subconscious and is pretty sneaky—at least mine is).

3: Communicate and Control Issues
To be able to trust someone else will correctly do the delegated task, communicate clearly by:

a: Telling them you believe they can do the task.

b: Clarifying your expectations about the delegation (e.g., what you want and when you want it).

c: Giving them enough authority so they can do the work and letting everyone else involved know they have this authority.

d: Ensuring they know how to do the task (have they been adequately trained?) or they know where to get help (from you or others).

e: Agreeing on regular progress checks while the task is being done (you don't get to walk completely away from the task—unless you like the possibility of an unmitigated disaster—but this doesn't mean breathing down their neck! Give them the space they need to do the job.) to ensure the task is understood and performed in an appropriate manner.

f: Determining with the delegate the criteria on which the outcome will be judged (and not insisting they do the job your way!).

g: Holding them accountable for the work they do by insisting on reasonable and required results—and not perfection.

4: The Value of Delegation to the Delegate

Delegation is about development, not dumping. Delegation should allow others to use and develop their skills and knowledge. Each task delegated should have enough complexity to stretch the delegate's skill set. Do not make decisions when the delegate is capable—when they present a problem, they must also present a solution to the problem.

5: Celebrate and Praise!

When the task has been successfully completed, recognize the delegate and celebrate their success—then give them more stuff to do!

Still having trouble delegating? Then consider this:

Determine how much your time is actually worth (divide annual compensation by the number of hours worked per year, then divide the number of hours worked per year by sixty to determine the dollar amount of every minute you work).

When you perform work someone else can do, you are "wasting" the value of your time by the length of time it takes you to complete that work.

Stop doing that!

Delegation frees you up to do more important work—and it empowers the person to whom you delegate, too! Could there possibly be a better win-win?

DO NOT DO LIST

The Power of the "Do Not Do List"

"The common man is not concerned about the passage of time. The man of talent is driven by it." —Schopenhauer

I love the Daily To Do List! It is my favorite Personal Productivity habit and something I do automatically at the end of each day. This simple approach is still the most effective Personal Productivity tool and, when used consistently, increases productivity by 20%, while reducing stress and saving energy.

While I strongly recommend the Daily and Weekly To Do Lists to everyone I coach, I believe a more powerful tool to generate greater Personal Productivity is the Do Not Do List! This is the list that stops you from doing those things that don't move you toward accomplishing your goals.

Some simple rules for creating an effective Do Not Do List are:

1: Start by creating a Weekly To Do List. Use stream of consciousness mode and list every work item you are going to attempt to do in the next seven-day period.

2: From the Weekly To Do List, create four other lists using the following criteria:

List #1: Tasks nobody should be doing.
It's amazing how some tasks continue to be done even though they have outlived the Return On Investment of time, energy and resources it takes to do them. Examine each task on your list carefully and determine if the time has come to eliminate a task altogether. And "we have always done it that way" is not a good reason to continue to do something!

List #2: Tasks you want to do but don't need to do.
Everybody has certain tasks they really enjoy doing and, at one time, probably moved them towards their goals. But if these tasks are no longer moving you toward achieving your current goals, time to say bye-bye.

List #3: Tasks better performed with technology.
Workplace technology should exist for only one reason: to make your work life easier. Find out if there is technology that you are unaware of that can be used to either eliminate tasks or make them easier to perform. Determine if a certain application of technology is worth the agony of the initial learning curve by calculating the long-term ROI of the initial investment of time, energy and resources before deciding to make the investment.

List #4: Tasks other people can do as well as or better than you.
If someone can do a task as well as you can or better than you can, delegate it already!

3: Remove all of the tasks on Lists #1 through #4 from your Weekly To Do List and at the end of every workday review your Daily To Do List for the next day to make sure none of the tasks on Lists #1 through #4 are on the Daily To Do List.

Now repeat the process by finding more tasks to put on the Do Not Do List!

THE MORNING MANTRA

09

Feeding the Brain for Fun and Productivity!

"The belly rules the mind." —Spanish Proverb

Why focus on food when wanting to increase productivity? Because food + liquids = fuel for the brain. To be productive, we need to fuel our brain, whose cells require two times the energy of the other cells in the body. To keep our brain working effectively and efficiently throughout the day, the brain's energy level must be kept high enough so that it doesn't become stressed or succumb to exhaustion, and reduce our level of productivity. Here's how to provide your brain with the right fuel to keep it (and you) at your most productive level for the entire workday:

Coffee and More Coffee: I love coffee! My mind barely functions and the creative juices don't flow in the morning until I have my first couple of swigs of a grande latte with an extra shot of espresso. Then, to keep the ideas flowing, I brew a pot of coffee for the rest of the morning. To be able to perform at a high level during my four hours of teaching from 6:00 p.m–10:00 p.m., I get a grande iced double shot—four shots of espresso—in the afternoon. Dynamite! At one time, the medical community would have predicted a short life span for a caffeine consumer like me, but no more. Research shows that not only does caffeine improve productivity by causing feelings of well-being, it also increases energy, alertness, focus and motivation, and it reduces the risk of dying early from a heart attack or stroke. So, if your blood pressure will allow it, enjoy another cup of guilt free coffee!

Mother Still Knows Best: Your mother knew breakfast was the most important meal of the day. You know it, too. If you don't feed the brain in the morning, it becomes confused and slows down. And we don't want that, do we? But you still don't eat breakfast! Here's the simplest way to get the benefits of breakfast and keep the brain (and Mom) happy: eat fruit for breakfast and get the complex carbohydrates that break down gradually, releasing glucose (which your body converts to energy) to fuel the brain during the entire morning.

Let's Do Lunch: Lunch needs to replenish the glucose-energy level being drained by your brain's continuous mental exercise. That means no fast foods and heavy lunches (i.e., steak and potatoes), which reduce the brain's ability to function at a high level. I save those items for dinner, when I can afford to be stupid. Instead, have a vegetable salad, which provides much of the same benefits as fruit. Adding an egg provides choline that boosts brainpower by making the signals to nerve cells in the brain faster. Fish is also good lunch item because it contains Omega-3 fatty acids, which builds gray matter and generates emotional balance and a positive attitude. So, cut the crap food at lunch!

Guilt Free Snacking: Feeding your glucose level with fruit throughout the day provides the brain with the continual flow of glucose-energy it needs to function at a high level. Now you have no reason to experience that afternoon lull in energy and productivity.

Be a Sponge Bob Square Pants: Proper hydration is essential for optimal brain functioning since liquids reduce the stress hormones that fatigue and slow down the brain. To adequately water the brain, drink 80 ounces of water and/or fruit and vegetable juices a day. Skip the soft drinks, because the sugar content causes cells to suck glucose from the brain, leaving it without energy, which reduces your ability to focus and think properly. Duh!

An increase in the foods and liquids that keep your brain running on high will enhance your brainpower and your productivity! So, wait until after work to indulge your inner Big Mac and suck down that sixty-four ounce Slurpee.

Wow! This Mantra has drained my brain—time to get another jolt of joe.

$\underset{\text{THE}}{\text{MORNING}}$ MANTRA

10

The Energizer Bunny Effect

"Nothing is so contagious as enthusiasm."
—Samuel Taylor Coleridge

There are three essential ingredients necessary for high performance: adequate resources, proper time management and a high level of energy. If an individual or organization possesses these three ingredients in the proper amount, a high level of performance is virtually guaranteed.

While everyone acknowledges the need for adequate resources and proper time management, very few people are aware of the need for a high level of energy, even though anecdotally, we know this to be true. Now, there is research to support the idea that energy is essential to high performance. Dr. Will Felps, a Rotterdam Business School professor, estimates that teams with just one "deadbeat" or "downer" (which I define as "Energy Sucks"—those who leave others drained of energy and enthusiasm by exhibiting negative thoughts and feelings and then transferring their negativism to other employees) suffer a performance disadvantage of 30–40% when compared to teams that have none. Most successful high-performance teams have a large number of "Energizers"—people who exhibit high levels of energy and optimism about the future and engage positively with other team members.

In this regard, the level of energy that managers create and display definitely affects those employees around them. Managers are always "on stage," continually being scrutinized by the Workforce from the time they arrive at the workplace until they leave. Because of their impact on others, managers must maintain and display a high level of energy as they interact with employees to engender optimism and enthusiasm about the work and the organization. Since energy, or the lack thereof, has such an impact on productivity, every Workplace Leader needs to be aware of the need for energy in the workplace and do what is necessary to ensure its presence at all times. Here are six rules to generate the necessary level of energy in any workplace:

Rule #1: Begin by hiring "Energizers"—people who have and display energy and enthusiasm.

Rule #2: Recognize it is your obligation to generate the required amount of energy in every situation.

Rule #3: Remember that *actions determine behavior*—act enthusiastically, and you will become energetic.

Rule #4: Pass energy along by positively interacting with and engaging other employees.

Rule #5: Give individuals an energy boost by recognizing them for good work.

Rule #6: Periodically purge the system of the Energy Sucks! Research shows that the impact of negative interactions with others in the workplace is five times stronger than positive interactions. No organization can truly tolerate the existence of Energy Sucks (aka "The Others")—they are toxic employees who negatively affect productivity and profitability. Get rid of them.

If none of these rules work, you can always invest in something else—a lot of espresso machines!

THE MORNING MANTRA

11

EXERCISE

Exercise Increases Productivity!

"Mens sana in corpore sano" (a sound mind in a sound body)
—Roman Motto

While I have always realized the physical benefits of exercise, I used to hate the amount of time it took! Now I engage in some form of physical exercise after every 90 minutes in the workday. Why the change in attitude and behavior? After doing research on how exercise improves productivity and attitude, I concluded *not* exercising is the real time waster! Research on the effects of exercise on productivity finds that an employee who exercises during the workday improves their job performance by 15% because:

Their energy level is higher.

Their time management skills are better.

Their mental sharpness, creativity, concentration and problem solving skills are improved.

They have a more positive attitude about work and their colleagues.

They have less stress and feel calmer.

Their productivity is greatest immediately after exercising.

Studies also show that lack of exercise negatively affects memory function, learning ability, attention span, abstract thought process, perceptual ability and creativity. Now that you are convinced as to the productivity benefits of physical activity (you really are, aren't you?), here are some ideas about how to become more physically active at work and enjoy the resulting productivity and health benefits:

1: Take the stairs instead of the elevator.

2: Sit on an exercise ball instead of a chair to strengthen your abs and back.

3: Get off your butt every 90 minutes and walk around.

4: Use the restroom on another floor and take the stairs to get to it.

5: Use a pedometer and walk 6,000 to 10,000 steps a day.

6: Get a headset for your phone so you can move around while you talk.

7: Keep dumbbells in your desk drawer and exercise while on the phone.

8: Take a heart-pumping walk with a co-worker instead of going out for lunch.

Be creative. Any movement is better than none. The latest trend in keeping fit at work is "micro office workouts", short three- to five- minute workouts you can fit in throughout the workday. A micro office workout can be stretches for arms, wrists and back (the body parts that suffer most from sitting and typing all day), or some basic strength training exercises done while sitting or standing at your desk.

There is always an excuse for not exercising, including my favorite: "I don't have time!" So cut the crap, start moving around and get more productive! Got to go—it's time for a micro walk.

THE MORNING MANTRA

12

GOALS

Your Tipping Point

"How do you eat an elephant? One bite at a time." —Bill Hogan

The Tipping Point, a book by Malcolm Gladwell, is subtitled "How little things can make a difference." It explores how ideas, products, services and social conditions start out small, build until they reach "the tipping point", and then become HUGE. I believe this same theory applies to Goal Setting.

The definition of a goal is "a clear, precise, written objective, with a set timeframe for completion." Without the writing and the timeframe, there is no goal; there is only a "dream." While there is nothing wrong with dreams, they won't take us where we want to go unless we turn them into concrete goals. A goal must also be difficult, but not impossible, to achieve—it must exceed a person's grasp but not their reach (example of impossible to achieve: just because I have a terrific jump shot doesn't mean I'll ever play for the Chicago Bulls since I am an old guy with bad knees!). A worthwhile goal requires a series of efforts to close "The Gap"—that space between the place where we are and the place we want or need to be. Seldom can worthwhile goals be achieved with a single effort. If that occurs, was the goal really "worthwhile" in the first place? As we move further along the path towards achieving the goal, the path often becomes easier until we reach "the tipping point." Suddenly, we're there—propelled by our own momentum and the cumulative power of "the little things that make a difference."

ar

Of course, if you don't take the first "bite" out of the Goal Setting Process—writing down your goals and establishing the Action Plan needed to accomplish them—you will never be able to finish eating the elephant. Also, you can't quit after the first few bites or when you hit "bones" (the inevitable obstacles between you and your goal). Any worthwhile goal requires persistence in the face of the inevitable adversity. Finally, being aware of the following reasons why worthwhile goals go bad will keep you focused on how you can reach "the tipping point":

Unrealistic Goals – Know the difference between possible and impossible!

Lack of Commitment – The goal must have meaning, and you must want it bad enough to do what needs to be done to achieve it!

Lack of a Tracking System – What gets measured gets done!

Lack of Accountability – Get an Accountability Buddy and publicly announce your goal!

Too Many Goals – Don't intensely focus on more than three goals at one time!

Lack of Support – Don't listen to those who say you cannot accomplish your goals!

I recently read that the Amish don't waste energy because they believe every action must have an understood purpose. I like that concept very much! So, does every action you take move you closer to your tipping point and achieving your goal, or are you wasting time and energy without a purpose?

THE MORNING MANTRA

13

The Value of Big Hairy Audacious Goals

"If you're going to be thinking, you may as well think big."
—Donald Trump

Ｗhile lounging in the sun on vacation in Cabo San Lucas, Mexico (on a speaking gig no less!), I reviewed management guru Tom Peters' concept of setting Big Hairy Audacious Goals (BHAG) and decided it was time to set a few BHAG of my own. As I wrote out my BHAG, I reflected on the importance of setting Big Hairy Audacious Goals and my take-aways on what Peters had to say:

Realistic goals are uninspiring! If the potential payoff is just average, your effort will be average. Your reach should always exceed your grasp!

The timing is never right to start Big Hairy Audacious Goals! Just Do It!

Don't reinvent the wheel! Find someone who has achieved what you want and ask them how they did it.

People will try to stop you before you get started! However, they will get out of your way when you start moving.

Be assertive without burning bridges! Accept advice graciously, even if you are not going to use it.

Concentrate on your strengths, not your weaknesses! Spending time, energy and resources on fixing weaknesses equals mediocre results.

Stress that pushes you beyond your comfort zone is healthy and stimulates growth!

Do not overestimate the competition or underestimate yourself! You are better than you think.

Failure is an option! But never let the thought of failure deter you.

While there will always be barriers to success, Big Hairy Audacious Goals provide the adrenaline rush to help you overcome the barriers to reaching that success.

THE MORNING MANTRA

14

Eliminating Bad Habits

"Good habits, once established, are just as hard to break as are bad habits." —Robert Puller

Eliminating a bad habit and replacing it with a good habit is a doable, but difficult, task. The key factor to success or failure in eliminating a bad habit is desire: How much do you want to change? This is the key to success or failure when it comes to changing behavior—which is what changing habits is all about. In order to change established habits, you really gotta want it bad.

How long does it take to eliminate a bad habit? Unfortunately, regardless of what you have heard, there is no time frame that determines when you have successfully eliminated a bad habit. It depends on the habit (talk to a smoker who is trying to quit!) and your desire to change. To eliminate a bad habit and improve your life, use the following process:

Identify the one habit you want to change: Only change one habit at a time. Trying to change more than one habit at a time is overwhelming and leads to failure.

Carefully define the bad habit you want to eliminate: Describe it, visualize the detrimental effect it has on your behavior and realize what triggers you and causes the bad habit to occur.

If possible, replace the bad habit with a good habit: Because focusing on the positive takes less effort and energy than focusing on the negative, eliminating a bad habit is easier when you are formulating a good habit to take its place. Set up a routine to go with the new habit. By establishing an environment in which the new habit will thrive, you can achieve the new habit at the expense of the bad habit.

Practice, Practice, Practice: New habits are developed by consistent and persistent practice. Without practice, until the new habit becomes firmly established, you will revert to the old habit.

Stick to the Plan, Stan! Every time you abandon the new habit and revert back to the old habit, you are starting over. The more times you start over, the harder it is to change.

Tell everyone about the new habit you are developing: Few of us make significant changes without the support of others, so tell people what you are trying to achieve and ask them to support the change. By having a strong support team, new habits are easier to achieve. Give regular progress reports about how you are doing to at least one person who is your designated Accountability Buddy.

As with anything worthwhile in life, eliminating bad habits takes hard work. However, the results—a more productive, enjoyable life—make the effort worthwhile.

15

Pardon the Interruptions!

"The average American worker has fifty interruptions a day, of which seventy percent have nothing to do with work."
—W. Edwards Deming

I don't handle interruptions well. Once focused on a task, I get very annoyed when interrupted. Yet, half my workday is devoted to handling interruptions! That is the average amount of time most of us spend dealing with interruptions every single workday! Obviously, interruptions are, and will remain, a HUGE part of everyone's workday. Instead of freaking out and continually whining about them, we need to accept interruptions as a fact of work life and build our Personal Productivity program around them. This means having the ability to deal effectively with them and still get the scheduled tasks on our daily To Do List done. You can survive interruptions and minimize their impact on your productivity by:

1: Getting your mind right by accepting interruptions as part of your job.

2: Identify recurring interruptions. Your time audit will reveal the pattern of the frequency, type and time of most interruptions.

3: Plan for recurring interruptions by anticipating their occurrence and scheduling important work around them by blocking out the time necessary to deal with them on your Daily To Do List.

4: Schedule times to check e-mails but no more than four times a day (making you sweat, aren't I?).

5: Schedule times to return phone calls. Let voicemail handle most calls.

6: Have meetings on your schedule rather than allow continual drop-ins.

7: Bunch related tasks together, and handle several at the same time.

8: Schedule focus time for important tasks when interruptions are not allowed.

9: Just say "No!" to unnecessary interruptions (easy to say, hard to do).

10: Learn to appropriately socialize at work. Too much of a good thing can become a bad thing.

11: After the interruption, train yourself to go right back to the task you were doing. Don't allow the effects of the interruption to linger.

12: Allow for an unexpected opportunity (e.g., your kids stop in at your office unannounced) and then screw the To Do List!

Now that you have interrupted your workday to read this—get back to work!

14 Reasons Why Meetings Suck and What to do About Them

"Meetings are indispensable when you don't want to do anything." —John Kenneth Galbraith

Why Meetings Suck and What to Do About That

1: There is no specific purpose for the meeting!

Since meetings can be used to avoid action, always ask: is this meeting necessary as a "call to action" or to re-energize a group? A meeting that does not produce action is a waste of time and resources. Avoid this by determining the meeting's specific outcome (a written pre-ordained purpose to be accomplished within a pre-determined time period) before scheduling it. There are only four reasons to hold a meeting:

- To solve a problem

- To make a decision

- To develop a plan

- To answer a question

2: A meeting is not the best way to accomplish the purpose!

Companies hold twice as many meetings as necessary. Once you know the meeting's purpose, ask if a meeting is the best way to accomplish that purpose. Hold a meeting only when it is important to have face-to-face interaction (i.e., a performance review or re-energizing a group). Giving instructions or checking on progress doesn't require a meeting, so, if that is the meeting's purpose, consider other methods of communication (e-mail, conference calls) instead of a meeting.

3: There is no agenda.

Every meeting needs a written agenda setting forth when the meeting begins and ends, every item to be discussed, who is required to be there for each item and a time limit for discussing each item. Also determine what action is needed, what problem gets solved, what decision gets made, what plan gets developed or what questions gets answered. Each attendee needs to have the agenda prior to the meeting. At the beginning of the meeting, review the agenda and the anticipated outcome.

4: There is no respect for everyone's time.

Set a time limit for the meeting. Start on time. Stay on time. End on time or, better yet, end early. Accomplish the meeting's purpose but in as little time as possible. To maintain focus and energy, no meeting should last longer than ninety minutes—unless food is provided!

5: No one is prepared!

Send out the agenda at least five workdays before the meeting so attendees can be adequately prepared to participate in the meeting. Attendees not adequately prepared must be held accountable.

6: There are unnecessary people in the meeting.

The bigger the group, the less likely the meeting will be productive. Keep meetings as small as possible (five to eight people) by only having attendees who are necessary to accomplish the meeting's purpose. A meeting doesn't require an audience: attendees should be there only when needed, and they should leave when they have made their contribution.

7: Attendees are not focused on the meeting's agenda.

The meeting leader is tasked with moving the meeting forward and keeping all attendees focused on the agenda. If someone starts discussing an item not on the agenda or out of the determined order, the meeting leader needs to refocus the meeting on the proper agenda item. This means attendees don't have handheld devices and laptops in the meeting, there are no side conversations and there is no interrupting or disrespectful behaviors. Since the participants' energy is low at the beginning of a meeting, rises at the middle and declines at the end, begin a meeting with announcements, followed by action items that lead to decisions.

8: One attendee monopolizes the meeting.

No one should speak for more than five minutes on an agenda item. If someone tries to monopolize the meeting or goes off on a tangent, they need to be re-focused by the meeting leader.

9: Most attendees aren't participating.

Participants need to feel the meeting is a safe environment where they can be candid enough to express useful ideas. By directly asking people to participate, the leader establishes this safe environment.

10: PowerPoint presentations are long and boring.

Don't use PowerPoint. Instead, use a flip chart.

11: Give us a break already!

Attendees need a twenty-minute break every ninety minutes (fifteen minutes for the bathroom and checking e-mail and phone calls, and five minutes to be physical).

12: There is no summary.

Have someone other than the meeting leader take notes about what decisions were made, problems solved, plans developed, questions answered and future actions to be taken—by when and by whom. Within seventy-two hours after the meeting, the meeting leader should create a one-page Meeting Summary/Action Plan and send it to the attendees and others who need to know what occurred at the meeting.

13: There is no debrief.
Take several minutes at the end of a long meeting to determine how to make the next meeting shorter and more productive.

14: There is no follow-up.
The meeting leader must follow up to ensure every attendee knows his or her part in the Action Plan and to ensure the Action Plan is implemented. The leader then determines if another meeting is necessary.

If you have any of these meeting time wasters inflicted on you, scream about it until they stop!

The Real Cost of Holding a Meeting that Sucks

One reason companies tolerate Meetings That Suck is that they don't realize how much a sucky meeting really costs. By calculating a meeting's true costs, we can see that Meetings That Suck cost more in lost productivity than any ROI they can possibly generate and, hopefully, this information will help stop the madness of Meetings That Suck.

To calculate the direct cost of a meeting, multiply the number of attendees by the attendees' hourly wages, and then multiply that number by the hours the meeting lasts. Do this for a twelve-month period for all the company's meetings and you may have The Big One.

While you'll be unpleasantly surprised at the direct cost of all those meetings, don't forget to add in the hidden costs of Meetings That Suck. The next three indirect costs can be difficult to determine, but to calculate the real cost of every Meeting That Sucks, they must be included:

- **Cost of Lost Productivity after the Meeting That Sucks** or the amount of time it takes attendees to refocus on other tasks after the meeting. My estimate: 10% of the time the attendee spends in these meetings.

- **The Lost Opportunity Cost of a Meeting That Sucks** is the value of the next best task you couldn't perform because of attending the Meeting That Sucks. The Lost Opportunity Cost is determined by what each of the attendees would have done with the time they spent in the Meeting That Sucks. My estimate: loss of 5% of the organization's total revenue stream.

- **A Meeting That Sucks is an Energy and Attitude Black Hole** that generates fatigue and negative attitudes when attendees can't answer the questions, "Why was I there?" and "What did we accomplish?" My estimate: 5% of the organization's total revenue stream.

When you realize how much Meetings That Suck really cost the organization, it should be a no-brainer to make every meeting as productive and efficient as possible. Here are a few more suggestions to make your meetings more tolerable and productive:

1: Hold short meetings (less than thirty minutes) standing up.

2: Keep the meeting room cool to heighten alertness.

3: Provide energy snacks and water for meetings in excess of ninety minutes.

4: Schedule meetings in thirty-minute increments instead of sixty-minute increments (e.g., instead of scheduling a two-hour meeting, have a ninety-minute meeting).

5: Schedule meetings immediately before lunch and quitting time.

Remember, a non-sucky meeting is one where the attendees leave thinking, "This was a good use of my time."

THE MORNING MANTRA

MIND POWER

Some Random Thoughts About Mind Power

"Effective Time Management is the best-kept secret of the rich."
—Jim Rohm

As a part of my frequent travel routine, I load up on magazines for the flight. I enjoy magazines like *Wired, Fast Company,* and *Success*—quick reads that provide nuggets of information I can research further and use in my personal and/or professional life. During my last trip, the five magazines I read each contained an article about the power of the mind. Since I believe in the ability of an individual to achieve their goals if they believe they can and are willing to impose the self-discipline necessary to do the hard work that leads to success, I like to see this concept validated by hard facts. Some facts about mind power contained in the magazines were:

> **1:** Two groups of patients are given the same drug. One group of patients is told the drug cost $2.80 a pill, while the other group is told the drug cost 10 cents a pill. The group that thinks the drug was more expensive showed greater physical improvement than the other group. The interesting thing: the "drugs" for both groups were placebos! Medical research suggests at least 30% of successful medical treatments occur because the patient believes the treatment will work and, based on that belief, the body will release endorphins to relieve pain and improve the person's medical condition.

2: The human brain, like a computer, does not know the difference between the truth and what people tell it. The mind will believe what you tell it to believe. By programming your mind in a positive way, you can get positive results.

3: The body will respond to mental input as if it were physically real. Brain scans reveal that when a person imagines an event, the area of the brain that would be activated during the actual physical event will light up. Visualize success and you can become successful.

The power of the mind applies to every activity in your life, including Personal Productivity. However, to achieve control of your Personal Productivity, you have to believe you can achieve control of it! If you continue to think there are too many obstacles (customers, bosses, too much to do) between you and increasing your Personal Productivity, you will be correct. Your attitude will determine your destiny.

THE MORNING MANTRA

MIND POWER

Fixed versus Growth Mindset

"Whether you think you can or can't, you're right." —Henry Ford

I have experienced the Power of Mindset in my own business. In 2008, the economy collapsed and took my training and development business with it. After all, after my clients laid off 50% of their employees, there wasn't a need for training! Forced to examine the future of my business, I realized I needed to change the focus of my consulting practice. While executive and business coaching and organizational restructuring had always been a part of my practice, they had not been my sole focus.

After the realization my focus had to change, I began to educate myself more fully in these areas and to develop programs to meet the needs of my clients as they responded to the new challenges of the Knowledge Economy. Over a twelve-month period, I reinvented my practice by honing my existing skill sets and developing new ones. The ability to view existing opportunities from a Growth Mindset rather than a Fixed Mindset allowed me to survive the WorkQuake™ of the Knowledge Economy and a devastatingly bad economy.

I am a HUGE believer that the Power of Mindset should be applied to all aspects of one's life. Moreover, I, like Henry Ford, believe a person's mindset is the primary indicator of success or failure when it comes to workplace performance. Yes, I know there are always external barriers that can stop even the most positively minded person (I don't care how good your jump shot is, at 50+ you're not playing guard for the Chicago Bulls!) from succeeding. However, I also know without the proper mindset, there don't have to be external barriers to stymie success because the internal barriers will be sufficient to guarantee failure.

Now there is scientific research—presented in *Mindset: The New Psychology of Success* by Carol S. Dweck, a professor of psychology at Stanford University—to support Henry Ford's and my position. In her book, Dweck poses the very important question, "What separates people who perform consistently well from those who don't?" She believes it is whether a person has a Fixed Mindset or Growth Mindset. She contends the Growth Mindset is the mindset for success, because people who have a Growth Mindset don't believe success is based on their talent (even though having talent is a good thing!). Rather, they continually develop their talent, viewing themselves as a work in progress. More importantly, when people with Growth Mindsets fail, they don't give up. Since their tendency is to learn and grow from every challenge, after experiencing a failure, they look for ways to perform better in the future because they believe they can. People who have a Growth Mindset know that effort is the main way to obtain necessary knowledge and create new skill sets.

In contrast, Fixed Mindset individuals believe people are born talented or smart, or they're not. Success for people with a Fixed Mindset depends very little on continuing development and learning because it doesn't matter. They believe either people have what it takes to succeed or they don't. If they don't, there is no way to change their lot in life. When those with a Fixed Mindset are faced with circumstances requiring they change their approach, they often fail and then don't think about ways to improve. Instead, they hide behind the "this is the way we have always done it" mantra because further risk exposes them to additional failure.

Fortunately, intelligence is not fixed. It is learnable, changeable and even teachable. Because our limitations are learned and set by ourselves, anyone who chooses to do so can develop the Growth Mindset. Even though I continue to have my doubts about some people!

MULTITASKING

Multitasking:
Just Don't Do It!

"Multitasking—screwing everything up simultaneously."
—Unknown

Many people remain convinced they can do several tasks competently at the same time. While this sounds good, it isn't true. What really matters if you truly want to be productive is not just showing up, but also actually "being present in the moment". This means giving up our national pastime: multitasking. I define multitasking as doing at least two things badly at the same time. And, regardless of what you may think, it's impossible to multitask and also be present in the moment—unless the task you are doing requires so little attention you can do it blind-folded and not lose a hand!

Still not convinced?

In my never-ending quest to convince others I'm right and they're wrong (at least about Personal Productivity issues), here is factual information about why you should not be a multitasker. Please stop texting and focus on reading it!

Studies show the human brain can only effectively perform one task at a time, even if the tasks being performed are very simple. We are not built to multitask, but to focus. When we force ourselves to multitask, we are less efficient in the long run, even though it can feel like we're being more efficient. A few quick facts:

A University of London research study found workers who multitask suffer a temporary reduction in IQ more than twice that found in marijuana smokers.

Jonathan Spira, an analyst at the business research firm Basex, estimates extreme multitasking costs the U.S. economy $650 billion a year in lost productivity.

Research finds multitasking contributes to the release of stress hormones and adrenaline, which can cause long-term health problems and contributes to short-term memory loss.

A 2009 research study from Stanford University, *Proceedings of the National Academy of Science*, notes that:

- Multitaskers are lousy at everything

- Multitaskers don't focus as well as non-multitaskers

- Multitaskers are weaker at shifting from one task to another than non-multitaskers

- Multitaskers are more distractible than non-multitaskers

- Multitaskers are weaker at organizing information than non-multitaskers

- Habitual multitaskers are even worse at multitasking than people who don't ordinarily multitask

Here are a few signs to determine if someone is multitasking:

- They take a phone call in the middle of your conversation or put you on hold.

- They merely nod or grunt and don't engage by asking a question or making a comment.

- They don't turn away from their computer while speaking to you on the phone (and, yes, the person on the other end of the call knows you are on the computer and barely paying attention to them! Very rude!).

While it isn't easy being present all the time, letting someone know you're listening—*really* listening—could be the biggest boon to your career and personal relationships possible.

Multitasking is all about NOT paying attention and the failure to exercise judgment about what is really worthy of our attention. On the other hand, Personal Productivity requires a finely honed skill for paying attention and not multitasking. It's always your choice. Choose wisely and stop multitasking already!

Nature versus Nurture – There May Be a Winner

"Genes and family may determine the foundation of the house, but time and place determine its form." —Jerome Kagan

I enjoyed reading Jeff Colvin's *Fortune* magazine article, *"Why Talent is Overrated,"* because I believe every employee is a "talented" employee who can make a big difference to an organization's success by producing extraordinary results—if they are properly trained, coached and mentored.

Colvin, the author of *Talent Is Overrated: What Really Separates World-Class Performers from Everybody Else*, posits that great performance doesn't come from innate talent (nature) but from intense "deliberate practice" (nurture). Instead of doing the things we are good at (our strengths), we must seek out the areas where we're not so good (our weaknesses). After each work activity, we should have others (coaches or mentors) tell us exactly what we didn't do as well as we could have, so we can train additionally or practice the activity. After receiving this constructive feedback, the next time we perform the activity, we'll be more proficient at performing it (similar to improving your golf game with the help of a teaching pro).

"Deliberate practice" continually stretches an employee just beyond their comfort zone by identifying the difficult activities required to improve performance and then doing those activities over and over. The important thing to note is the focus of this approach is on improvement, not failure. Colvin suggests individual employees can achieve high performance without the employer's involvement through self-regulation before work (setting immediate goals to be accomplished during the day), during work (close self-observation of their actions) and post-activity (comparing their performance against someone who does it better and adapting). However, he notes, to be most effective, "deliberate practice" requires a coach or mentor to design those difficult activities and provide accurate feedback about performance.

Unfortunately, most employers either aren't aware of or ignore these fundamentals of creating great employee performance. Those employers, intent on thriving in the WorkQuake™ of the Knowledge Economy, must provide their Core Employees with continual training, coaching and mentoring so they can implement "deliberate practice" and achieve individual and team greatness in the performance of their daily work activities, helping the organization achieve a huge advantage over competitors in the marketplace.

However, the process of "deliberate practice" is an investment: the cost is high immediately and the ROI comes later. Those employers who believe the source of great employee performance is in the nurturing of Core Employees will make this investment. As for the other companies, the dustbin of history is full of companies who rely on nature to take its course.

THE MORNING MANTRA

21

NIGHT OWLS

The Night Owl Syndrome

*"Night time is really the best time to work. All the ideas are
there to be yours because everyone else is asleep."*
—Catherine O'Hara

I recently read an article about the struggles of Night Owls (41% of Americans who are more productive during the evening) trying to comply with their company's standard work schedule. Even though they are required to show up at work in the morning, they don't become really productive until later in the day. This irritates their bosses and co-workers, who are mostly Morning Larks (what a sweet sounding name!) and, as the name implies, are most productive during the morning. Research establishes we have little control over whether we are Morning Larks or Night Owls (that damn genetic thing again!). However, here are some creative solutions companies and employees can implement to address this issue and increase overall organizational productivity:

1: A Single Starting Time Is So Industrial Age!
Is it really necessary to have everyone start at the same time? Flexible starting times let people start their workday when they are most productive.

2: Compromise!
If everyone must start work at the same time, compromise by scheduling team meetings and project work at a middle ground time,

taking into account the needs of both the Morning Larks and the Night Owls.

3: Schedule Important Work When You Are Most Productive!

I am a Morning Lark who is up by 5:00 a.m. (if Starbucks opened any earlier, I would be up earlier!). If possible, I do all my creative work by 11:00 a.m. Then, as my energy level drops, I start doing the more routine stuff (mailings, telephone calls, e-mails, exercise). Don't fight your genetic inclinations! To increase your level of productivity, determine what period of the day you are most productive, and schedule your work into that time period.

In the Knowledge Economy, where we count on people to be innovative and creative, we need to take into account each person's individual differences and needs whenever possible, and provide the flexibility and environment needed to increase each employee's potential and contribution to the organization. When making these accommodations, remember: what's good for the employee is often good for the organization!

THE MORNING MANTRA

22

ORGANIZING

Dealing With Disorganization!

"Control the controllable and attempt to understand how to make the uncontrollable controllable." —Jim Rohn

U pon my return from conducting a Performance Improvement Workshop in Savannah, Georgia, the mess my office was in stunned me. It looked like someone had ransacked it! The problem: I can never stop making last-minute improvements to the customized workbooks I create for each workshop, so until the last minute before I left for the airport, I was improving the material. Upon my return, it was apparent my office was in a state of serious disorganization!

Rather than jam all the material into a convenient cabinet drawer until the next workshop on that topic, I decided to engage in some overdue office reorganization. Why? Because continually pawing through stuff piled up on every work surface is a waste of time (it is estimated thirty-eight hours each year per employee is lost looking for misplaced items!) and very frustrating, so these are the steps I followed to return my office to a state of organization:

> **1:** I completely cleared off my desk by putting everything into one BIG pile. Just being able to see the top of my desk made me feel better!

2: While I was in the process of piling, I got rid of unimportant stuff (e.g., magazines already read, unnecessary copies) by pitching it into the garbage can I moved next to my desk.

3: I then determined where everything needed to go by dividing the big pile into smaller piles of related stuff (i.e., magazine articles, workshop material, project proposals) and created space to accommodate each pile of related stuff if it didn't already exist (i.e., folder for billing, folder for specific workshop material, a box for extra newsletters). I now had a specific place for everything in my office.

4: I put the piles into the places I had assigned for them (i.e., storage cabinet, folder or box). The everyday stuff (e.g., stapler, printer paper) I relocated for easy accessibility. In addition, I kept throwing stuff out as I relocated items.

I felt good when I finished—and I could still see the top of my desk! So, I rewarded myself for a job well done by getting another Starbucks!

This process is not rocket science, but it does require: 1) awareness that disorganization is not a good thing, 2) time and patience to develop a system, and 3) discipline to stick to that system. I have provided some helpful hints to get you started on your own office disorganization, but everyone develops their own system once they start. The point is to develop a system that eliminates time wasted by continually having to look for or work around stuff. Give it a shot and feel The Good!

THE MORNING MANTRA

23

Organizing the Unorganized

"God, please bless this mess!" —Unknown

I believe effective Personal Productivity is partially based on how effectively we deal with the stuff that moves into our lives on a daily basis. Because of my personality type (some would describe it as anal; I call it having a curious mind), I am constantly collecting information about things in which I have an ongoing interest (Personal Productivity) or stuff that is only of momentary interest (how to plant Japanese maples—my boys got me one for Father's Day). To satisfy my lust for information, I collect articles from newspapers, magazines, websites, mailings, etc. By the end of the week, I have a pile of paper stacked next to the printer. The issue then becomes what to do next.

To keep from driving myself crazy with information overload, I have a system to keep the stuff collected in order. Without a workable system, the ability to benefit from the collected stuff diminishes dramatically. Frustration ensues when I waste time looking through stuff for the item I know is there but can't find. If you collect information like I do (and you should!), then an investment of two hours to develop a system to quickly sort through and save relevant information will yield a BIG return on your efficiency and productivity.

First, not everything you collect should be kept (we don't want that hoarder thing to rear its ugly head!). On Sunday morning, I move the pile to my desk and, with my trusty shredder turned on, I quickly go through the pile and destroy the stuff that, on second viewing, doesn't have enough value for me to keep. Anyone who wants to be better organized needs a good shredder! There is nothing like a good shredding buzz to start the day off right, before I start to collect more stuff by reading the Sunday papers!

Second, I go through the pile again. This time I sort the stuff into smaller piles of defined areas of interest (blogging, marketing, restaurants, etc.).

Third, I place all the smaller piles into the designated place for each identifiable topic. Articles go into labeled folders; interesting recipes (has anyone ever really eaten a quail's egg on toast?) go into a three-ring binder (never cook most of them, but I do like to read them occasionally); and visually interesting stuff goes onto a corkboard, strategically placed so I can see it during the day.

Fourth, there are always items that defy categorization, which I place into an "of interest file." (A *New York Times* article on Megalopolis: did you know Tokyo has thirty-five million inhabitants?). Every month, I go through this file and cull out the stuff that no longer trips my trigger.

Fifth, religiously follow your system. Make it a weekly routine. Skip a week and don't sort, cull or file and the pile quickly becomes a paper monster that will not stop growing and aggravating you.

To get the most out of your busy life, you need to develop systems and routines that make daily living more enjoyable. This leaves you time for the good stuff—like sitting under a Japanese maple!

$\underset{\rule{0pt}{0pt}}{\overset{\rule{0pt}{0pt}}{\text{THE}}}$ MORNING
MANTRA

24

The Money Set

"Perseverance is the hard work you do after you get tired of doing the hard work you already did." —Newt Gingrich

Anyone who lifts serious weights knows that the third set of repetitions of any exercise is called "The Money Set"—the part of the lifting process where you lift until you reach muscle failure. Why expend so much effort during The Money Set? Because that is the part of the process where you generate the greatest muscle and strength growth.

The opportunity to generate maximum results during The Money Set makes it imperative you give your undivided attention and utmost effort to every detail of every lift, concentrating on your form as much as on the amount of weight you are lifting. Add to that focus the concept of lifting until failure—until you can't lift the weight anymore—and you have the formula for a successful Long-Term Project (any project that takes you and your team four times as long to complete as a normal project).

Just as lifting weights consists of three sets, I contend that any Long-Term Project has three stages:

1: The "I'm Pumped!" Stage.
Like every serious weightlifter who is pumped up to begin lifting, everyone on the Long-Term Project team feels fresh, excited and enthusiastic about the possibilities and opportunities contained in the development and planning phase of a new Long-Term Project.

2: The "I'm Getting Tired!" Stage.

If the appropriate amount of effort and energy has been put into the lifting process, by the second set of repetitions the lifter has expended a lot of energy. He or she is beginning to experience fatigue, as well as mental doubts—especially with a third set of weights remaining. Similarly, the Long-Term Project team begins to feel the effects of effort and expenditure of energy associated with the implementation phase.

3: The Third Stage is the "Crap! Isn't this thing done yet?" Stage.

By this point, fatigue has set in, muscles are tired and the lifter's initial drive and enthusiasm have dissipated. The effort of the process takes its toll, and the lifter starts to think about quitting—letting the iron win. The Long-Term Project team is experiencing similar resistance to the completion of the project—the thousand details that have to be resolved. It makes the team consider short cuts and faulty processes—anything just to be done!

I contend the third stage is the most difficult stage of the Long-Term Project Process and the value of the project is in danger of being diminished. How do you stop the Third Stage from decreasing the value of the entire project? Or, to use gym-speak, how do you get your money out of The Money Set?

While not an inclusive list, since each Long-Term Project team is unique, the following weightlifting techniques can be applied to the completion stage so you are able to get all your money:

1: Be aware.

Just as every serious weightlifter knows when they pick up the first weight what to expect when they get to The Money Set, every team member needs to know, at the outset of a Long-Term Project, that the final stage will take a BIG toll on the team's enthusiasm and energy. This will make everyone on the team better prepared to cope when they begin the third stage.

2: No pain = No gain.

The only reason weightlifters endure the pain inherent in The Money Set is because they receive the payoff from the first two sets—and they know it. Similarly, every member of the team must realize that an important part of their effort through the first two stages will be lost unless they complete the job.

3: Become a little bit mental!

Because of the effort involved in "getting all your money" out of The Money Set, when your muscles don't want to willingly participate, it helps to get a little mental. Forcing the body to push beyond where it wants to go. Ditto with the Long-Term Project team. The first time you see The Completion Stage begin to take its toll, get a little bit crazy (and don't pretend you can't do crazy!), and infuse that dose of adrenaline and energy necessary to complete the project.

Now go get your money!

⊤HE MORNING ⊤ MANTRA

PLANNING

The Planning Process for 12 Months of Success

"Adventure is just bad planning." —Roald Amundsen

Step #1: Schedule three hours to plan the next twelve months.

Step #2: Go to an office supply store and pick up a twelve-month dry erase "at a glance" calendar and three colors of dry erase markers.

Step #3: Decide on your Free Days (vacation days, weekends, personal days, family days, goof-off days, get-personal-stuff-done days, etc.).

Step #4: Decide how many Strategy Days per month you need to work on your business. These are days for doing all the "important" but not urgent things like planning, strategizing, marketing and personal and professional development. I recommend at least one day per week.

Step #5: Choose a color for each of the following categories:

- **Free Day** – Color: _____

- **Strategy Day** – Color: _____

- **Working Day** – Color: _____ (the days remaining after determining Free Days and Strategy Days).

Step #6: Put your Free Days, your Strategy Days and your Working Days on the calendar.

Step #7: Once you have planned your year, make the following three commitments:

- Commit to fulfilling your Free Days with satisfying personal activities.

- Commit to working "on" your business during Strategy Days.

- Commit to making your business more successful during Working Days.

Now, take your first Free Day because you just earned it!

The Power of Prioritizing: Deciding What to Do Next

"Doing the right thing is more important than doing things right." —Peter Drucker

There is never—nor will there ever be—enough time to do all the things you have to get done during each workday. Tasks are infinite while time is finite (damn, reality bites, doesn't it?)! Is it better to spend your time contacting an existing customer or creating and sending marketing material to a prospect or working to improve your product? Should you have an hour meeting with your team or spend that hour returning phone calls instead?

The ability to decide what to do next—Prioritizing—is a skill set successful people develop and anyone can learn. Prioritizing is based on the fact that everything you do is not of equal value. Rather, 20% of the tasks on your daily To Do List will equal 80% of your productivity for the day (an application of the Pareto Principle—commonly called the 80/20 Rule). The trick is to identify the 20% of the tasks you need to do to get 80% of the Return On Investment (ROI) on your resources, time and energy. You do this by establishing Priorities—the order in which things get done—to determine which tasks you can eliminate, delay or delegate, based on the possible consequence of not doing those tasks at all or immediately. Deciding the important 20% of your daily activities, and doing them during your Productivity Cycle, will get you the greatest

ROI on your workday. Here are a few simple rules to start you down the path to becoming a Power Prioritizer and a more productive and successful person:

Decide what your goals are for the following day! Example: Are you going to concentrate on increasing sales or increasing profits? Or both? Without having daily goals, you cannot properly focus on achieving those goals. Then write those goals down! There is power in seeing your goals in written form. Put your goals in a place where you can see them all day long (I tape mine on the wall next to my desk—tough to miss them there).

Develop a daily "To Do List" aligned with achieving your goals for the day! The daily To Do List remains the most effective method of Personal Productivity. It is the easiest system to maintain and, if done properly, establishes what needs to be done to effectively manage your time (and if you are not managing your time, someone else is). Here is how I create my daily To Do List:

a: At the end of every workday, I go into stream of consciousness mode and write down every goal I want to accomplish the next day. The key word is *want*.

b: Next, I go down the list and divide it into "needs" and "wants." A "need" task left undone will cause detrimental aftereffects. Usually "wants" are easier to do; they are "busy work" or more fun. I move the "needs" to the top of the list and assign a priority number to each item, with #1 being the first item I need to get done the next day.

c: I then assign each "need" the amount of time I believe it will take for me to do it, starting with item #1. (Hint: "need" items usually require focused effort). When I reach twelve hours of activity, I stop, since that is when I cease working productively. The items left without a time (there are always some of those) may or may not go on my next day's To Do List, since I now have to re-think the necessity of doing them at all.

d: The following morning, I begin work by doing the #1 Priority item on my To Do List. No, I don't do the easy items first! There is one allowable exception to the Priority Rule: if you are not a "morning person" (I'm a morning person, up at 5:00 every morning—and it would be earlier if the local Starbucks would only open earlier, the slackers!), and the priority items require heavy duty focus and concentration, schedule them for the time of the day when you are most mentally alert.

e: When I finish each task on my To Do List, I record the actual amount of time it took me to do that task. Stunningly, there is often a big difference between the amount of time I thought it would take me and the amount of time I actually spent doing the task. Since I am an eternal optimist, my error is always in underestimating the amount of time it really took me to do the task! By comparing the amount of time it actually took me to accomplish the task to the amount of time I originally allocated for the task, the next time I perform that task or one similar, I am much more realistic about how much time it will take me. Through trial and error, I become better at managing my time, and my Personal Productivity improves.

Ask the following questions every ninety minutes during the workday (when you are taking a physical activity break from work!): Is what I'm doing moving me towards achieving my daily goal? Am I being productive or just active? At the end of the day, will I be satisfied with what I accomplished today?

At the end of the workday, measure the impact of the choices you made by determining how close you came to achieving your daily goals. Since every goal should be a "stretch goal," if you achieved all of your daily goals, you need to set more ambitious goals tomorrow.

If you made appropriate progress towards achieving your daily goals, reward yourself (a Starbucks coffee will do nicely, thank you!) for a job well done.

Repeat every day!

Simple, no? By Prioritizing, you complete fewer tasks, but the accomplished tasks are of higher value or return. What's not to like about that?

THE MORNING MANTRA

PROCRASTINATION

How to Stop Playing Procrastination—Don't Wait! Read this NOW!

"Someday is not a day of the week." —Unknown

The single biggest obstacle to success for most people is procrastination! Procrastination, or "deferring action," is the refusal to do what needs to be done when it needs to be done because a particular task is difficult, boring, time consuming, requires a tough decision or is not as much fun as doing something else.

How can I tell when I am procrastinating? Easy! I look at my Daily To Do List and at the items I continually move from one day's list to the next day's list. If an item shows up on five To Do Lists in a row, I know I'm playing procrastination with that task. Once I am aware of playing procrastination, I stop making excuses and immediately start doing that task. I have found that a delayed task never gets easier or goes away and is seldom as difficult or distasteful as I have mentally built it up to be. Once I start doing the task, I feel immediate mental relief, and my subconscious, which has been incessantly nagging me about getting the task done from the time I started to procrastinate, stops irritating me!

Nearly all of us suffer from procrastination, especially when faced with a task we either don't want to do or don't know how to do. However, according to research by Professor Joseph Ferrari of DePaul University in Chicago, procrastinators fall into three major categories. Which one describes you?

1: Arousal Procrastinators
Those who tackle projects at the last minute. They put work off because they believe they work best under pressure (studies show this is not true);

2: Avoidance Procrastinators
Those who routinely put off hard tasks just because they perceive them to be so overwhelming it's futile to even try to start them (however, they find once they start the task that it is easier than they thought); and

3: Decisional Procrastinators
Those who are so paralyzed by indecision or too much data ("analysis paralysis" or "over choice") that organizing thoughts and action is impossible.

So, how do you overcome procrastination of any kind? The only cure is to take these positive actions.

Determine If You Should Be Doing the Task! Doing tasks you don't have to do only provides an excuse for doing something other than what really needs to be done.

Admit You Are Procrastinating! Awareness is always the first step to making progress. Don't defend your procrastination habit by rationalizing why you are procrastinating!

Just Start! The most difficult part of many jobs is getting started. Don't wait for the "right mood" or "inspiration," or you'll never get the task done! Once begun, the task is often easier to do than expected. The two most important rules for overcoming procrastination: Rule #1: Get Started and Rule #2: Keep Going.

Get Organized! Do whatever is necessary to get your mind around the task. Create an Action Plan, make a list of resources needed to accomplish the task, and contact those people who are also involved in the task.

Have a Realistic Deadline! Allow adequate time to finish the task. If you don't have time to finish, request extensions on deadlines, get help from others, delegate tasks to others, and drop non-essential items from your schedule.

Break LARGE Projects Into Smaller Chunks! Break the task down into small pieces, assign a deadline to each chunk, and then complete the first chunk. Do smaller items first because this generates positivity and creates mental momentum. When you have finished a task, mark it off your list for visual confirmation you are making progress (you do have a list of items that must to be done—in priority order—right?).

Sometimes Good Enough Is Just Enough! Not every task requires perfection. Evaluate the requirements of the job to determine if it merits the investment of time and effort you are making.

Reward Yourself for Completing the Task! You get to choose your own reward for a job well done. I reward myself with an extra Starbucks when I have finished my daily drudgery.

Procrastination is a Major Killer of Good Ideas! Procrastination in two forms—a desire for perfection and doing something less important—is the primary reason why most good ideas are not implemented. Example: In a two-week period, I heard two great ideas. One concerns goats and the other a direct mailing campaign. Both ideas had merit and should have been implemented immediately. But the two people who had the ideas, and could definitely implement them, were procrastinating! They were waiting for "the right time" to begin. NOW IS ALWAYS THE RIGHT TIME TO BEGIN! Failure to implement a good idea NOW gives someone else the opportunity to beat you to the punch (You didn't really think you were the only one who could come up with that idea, did you?).

Here are a few rules to stop procrastination from killing your good idea:

Begin to implement your idea as soon as possible after your gut instinct tells you it will work. Immediately develop a one-page Action Plan containing the tasks and timeline necessary to take the idea to market!

Action—the enemy of procrastination—is more important than perfection! Don't waste time trying to perfect the idea! You don't know what is going to work until you put your idea into action!

Test the idea on your existing customers.

Balance your time between learning how to make the idea better and doing it.

Be prepared to eliminate the new idea if the marketplace tells you it is not working.

If the new idea is a keeper, improve it on the fly, as the marketplace tells you what it wants differently.

The goal is constant incremental improvement of the idea over time!

Now what are you waiting for?

PRODUCTIVITY

The 6 Basic Steps for Increasing Personal Productivity

"Work harder on yourself than you do on your job." —Jim Rohn

Since nearly everyone is interested in increasing their Personal Productivity, here are my Six Basics Steps for Improving Personal Productivity. Follow them and become a Master Manipulator of Time:

1: Awareness: Does Anybody Really Know What Time It Is?

Time is a non-renewable resource: Once it is spent, you cannot recover it. Most people are not in control of their Personal Productivity because they are not in control of their own time. Better management of your Personal Productivity requires you first be aware the problem is not a shortage of time but, rather, how you choose to use your time—after all, we all have the same 24 hours each day. If you want increased productivity, you need to change the way you choose to use your time by replacing existing bad habits with good habits. To begin this process, you must first identify your existing habits. Ready for the hard part? This requires that you keep a time log of all your activities for seven consecutive days. This is not an option! Without the time log, you can't accurately know where you are spending or wasting your time. Your time log will highlight time wasting activities and identify who is currently controlling your time. With this essential information, you can take the actions necessary to turn your bad Personal Productivity habits into good Personal Productivity habits.

2: Desire: You Gotta Want It Bad!

You must really *want* and *need* to change your habits or you will not stick to the Personal Productivity Action Plan long enough to reap its benefits. Before there can be meaningful change, you must decide: Do you really want to change? You will want to change only when you get a satisfactory answer to the question, "What is in it for me to change?" Only if you believe you will receive something more valuable than the amount of effort and aggravation created by the change process, will you invest the energy necessary to engage in the change process. So, now answer THE QUESTION: "Is taking control of your life by changing to good Personal Productivity habits worth the effort and energy it will take?" If the answer is an emphatic "Yes!" read on. If it is a tepid "Yes." go watch *The Biggest Loser*!

3: Knowledge: What You Don't Know Can Hurt You!

Based on reviewing the information contained in your time log, you can determine where your strengths and weaknesses are when it comes to Personal Productivity (Are you in too many useless meetings? Are you properly prioritizing your daily and weekly "To Do Lists"? Are you properly scheduling your day's activities? Are you procrastinating?). And you will discover who is really controlling your productivity (Are you properly delegating work? Are you allowing unimportant interruptions? Are you overwhelmed by paper?). Once you have established where you are "wasting" time (time spent that does not move you towards your Big Hairy Audacious Goals or maybe just towards the goals on your Daily To Do List), then you are ready to develop an Action Plan to eliminate your Personal Productivity weaknesses.

4: Action Planning: Does Man Really Plan and God Laughs?

Knowledge without action is a waste of (wait for it) TIME. Once you know what to do, develop a Personal Productivity Action Plan, with SMART Goal Setting to create direction and momentum. While everyone acknowledges how important it is to have a plan, most of us would rather "shoot from the hip" or "fly by the seat of our pants" than develop a written Action Plan. We prefer to race to the action steps—the Just Do It! Part—instead of the boring planning that precedes the action. Yet, without a written Action Plan, much of our time is wasted doing stuff that doesn't contribute to our achieving our goals. We are reactive, rather than proactive, to whatever happens around us, which means other people control our time. Planning gives you control over as much of your time as possible and is essential for improving Personal Productivity. Once you know what needs to be done to increase your Personal Productivity, you need to develop Personal Productivity Action Plans for your long-term (annual) and short-term (monthly, weekly, daily) goals.

Start with a Daily Action Plan—your strategy for proactively attacking the day—that includes priorities and time estimates and a realistic To Do List and a Do Not Do List (activities or tasks that don't move you towards your goals!), as well as specific action steps to achieve your goals.

After you are comfortable with the Daily Action Plan, develop Action Plans for the week, month and year. The key to a successful Action Plan is to plan both work and time by asking these five questions:

a: What do I expect to accomplish?

b: What will I have to do to achieve those accomplishments?

c: What are the priorities involved?

d: How much time will each activity require?

e: When will I do each activity?

5: Self-Discipline: Stick to the Plan, Stan!
Without the necessary long-term commitment of time and energy to stick to the Personal Productivity Action Plans (increasing Personal Productivity is a marathon, not a sprint), there will be no

improvement in your Personal Productivity. This type of commitment means developing the discipline—"want-power" in action—necessary to change. Think about something you wanted badly enough to change how you behave—losing weight by giving up fast food or saving for a vacation by not going to Starbucks (that is really wanting to change!). While turning bad habits into good habits is not easy, it is a necessary and ongoing process when it comes to improving Personal Productivity. If you want something badly enough, you will develop the discipline—the "want-power"—to do it. Consider these when developing discipline:

a: Flexibility.

Mike Tyson, the former ear-biting boxer, said, "Everyone has a plan until they get hit." And we all get "hit" with stuff (e.g., an unexpected work emergency) that wrecks our time management Action Plan for the day or the week. The flexibility to accept that those "hits" are inevitable creates the ability to get back on the time management track after having been knocked off it. Determine how much flexibility is needed for the unexpected in your daily and weekly time management Action Plan and build it into the Action Plan.

b: See Success.

Change your mental environment by visualizing exactly when, where and how you will do what allows you to accomplish your goal. Sound too freaking *New Age* for you? Consider: professional athletes improve their skills by visualizing the physical feat of shooting free throws, hitting a baseball or catching a pass. Discipline requires you begin to "see" success by imagining yourself being more productive. Imagine what to do to be more productive: closing your office door or going to Starbucks to get away from interruptions. Then become more disciplined by "seeing" a future where you have done what you need to do.

c: Seek Small Successes.

Faced with any task requiring discipline, our mind quickly moves to calculating the odds of success. The next thing we hear is that whiny internal voice telling us "the effort involved is just too great" or "you don't have what it takes to do what it takes, so stop this nonsense and go back to watching *American Idol*." Achieving goals requires we quiet the "monkey-chatter" inside our head and the best way to quiet our internal success blockers is to succeed. Small successes are the basis for the discipline we need to move onto greater successes. Start accomplishing big goals with small actions.

6: The Power of Accountability: Go Tell It On a Mountain!

Once you have established your Personal Productivity Action Plan, tell it to those who will support you in achieving your plan's goals. Tell them, in detail, what you want to do and when you are going to do it. Then find one person you respect, who supports your goals, make them your Accountability Buddy and, at least once a week, report your progress to that person.

Simple common sense stuff, no? But don't kid yourself. Each one of these 6 Steps is easy to talk about and easy to think about but very hard to implement (see Step #2).

THE MORNING MANTRA

29

PURPOSE

Purpose & the Personal Mission Statement

"Purpose is what gives life meaning." —Charles Perkhurst

Do you wake up in the morning energized for a new day of exciting possibilities, or do you get out of bed, dreading what the day will bring? Those who greet each day as an adventure have a guiding purpose in their lives and a proactive mindset ready to take action when opportunity presents itself. Stephen Covey (*The 7 Habits of Highly Effective People*) calls it a "personal mission statement." My Personal Mission Statement, written and placed where I see it throughout the day, keeps me on course. However, while I leave it unchanged from day to day, the methods I use to achieve my personal mission vary, depending on what unexpected challenges and opportunities cross my path.

Without awareness of our Personal Mission Statement, we remain unfocused, filling our day with "busy work"—stuff we think we have to do and that we substitute for meaningful and satisfying achievement. This meandering approach to life causes us to be perpetually dissatisfied and to wonder what is wrong and why we are not happier.

What Personal Mission Statement have you created to determine what you will say "yes" to each day because it moves you closer to your purpose and what you will say "no" to because it does not align with your purpose? Don't have a personal mission statement? Now is the perfect time to create one. I'm just saying!

THE MORNING MANTRA

30

How Has Your Week Gone?

"Anytime you suffer a setback or disappointment, put your head down and plow ahead." —Les Brown

How has your week gone? Were you able to fulfill all your commitments professionally and personally? Did you accomplish all the goals you set for yourself this week? Were you a Master Manipulator of Time?

Unfortunately, for most of us, at the end of the week, our daily and weekly To Do Lists look more like wish lists! Regardless of how committed we are to the process and regardless of how much effort we invest, at the end of the week, the results are often not what we anticipated. While this can be very discouraging, it is all part of the productivity cycle.

Anyone who succeeds at any meaningful project, initiative or undertaking, experiences setbacks on a regular basis. I experienced this in my recovery from double knee surgery. While I was making good progress towards full recovery, the process literally consisted of two steps forward and one step backward—two good days followed by one bad day. Very frustrating! This is the recovery process; there is no way to avoid it. When I stopped grousing and began to look at the daily progress I made, I realized, even with the one step backward, I was much further along towards my goal of full recovery than I was at the beginning of the week.

Successful people see this perpetual dance between progress and set-backs as an inherent part of the journey to success. Successful people DO NOT see setbacks as reasons to give up. They realize the only way to truly fail is to quit trying and stop doing.

We can't always move ahead as quickly as we would like. It usually takes much more time—and more effort—to succeed at something meaning-ful than we initially believe. When setbacks occur, we tend to think these are reasons to give up on our goals. Instead, view each setback as a new opportunity to refocus on your goals and get back to taking the action steps necessary to achieve your goals.

$\overline{\underset{\vdash}{\text{THE}}}$ MORNING MANTRA

31

You Are Getting Sleepy!

"The amount of sleep required by the average person is five minutes more." —Wilson Mizener

I used to hate sleep. What a waste of time! And the thought of taking a nap in the afternoon made me crazy (I put it in the same category as practicing yoga and taking vitamins). But that was then, and this is now.

After conducting plenty of research, both factual and anecdotal, I came to the conclusion a few years ago that both sleep and naps were essential elements of everyone's Personal Productivity—including mine. Why? Because during sleep, the body rests, rebuilds and restores, and the brain uses physical dormancy to recharge. Now, I already know your response: "*You* may not be able to, Oh Great Productivity Guru, but *I* can get along just fine on five hours of sleep per day. And besides, I have a Starbucks card, just in case."

That attitude is part of the problem: You cannot rely on your own sense of whether or not you're getting enough sleep because you are so chronically sleep-deprived that you consider it to be normal! You don't know what it feels like to be wide awake while you drink coffee, take a walk around the block or chat with co-workers trying to fight off sleep. However, even you can't fool Mother Nature for long, and your Personal Productivity and health are suffering every day you don't get between seven and eight hours of sleep. Here are some facts to convince you to start sleeping more:

- According to the National Sleep Foundation, 50% of Americans are sleep deprived.

- There is no substitute for sleep. Yoga and vitamins won't help! And neither will Starbucks!

- Sleep is cumulative—if you lose sleep one day, you feel it the next.

- Most experts agree the body and mind need between seven and eight hours of sleep per day.

- Sleep deprivation costs U.S. employers $18 billion each year in lost productivity.

- Getting less than seven hours of sleep per night decreases cognitive functioning (it makes you stupid!), the ability to perform complex tasks, creativity and memory, coping skills and immunity to diseases.

- Getting less than seven hours sleep per night also increases anxiety, weight gain, moodiness, aggressive behaviors, burnout, stress and the chances of having a heart attack.

- Even though you believe you can be more productive by sleeping less, you actually are more efficient and less irritable when you get the sleep you need.

- The quality and quantity of work is diminished by about 30% when an employee is sleepy.

- 51% of Americans report that sleepiness on the job interferes with the amount of work they get done. And 68% of adults say that sleepiness interferes with their concentration and increases the difficulty of handling stress on the job.

Finally, those of you who continue to think you can exist on five hours of sleep and still do a great job are probably the same individuals who thought they could pull an all-nighter and get an "A" on the chemistry exam—and we all know how that turned out!

THE MORNING MANTRA

32

STRESS

Harnessing Stress Energy!

"If you realized how powerful your thoughts are, you would never think a negative thought." —Pearce Pilgrim

Stress is unavoidable, but because of genes, personality and life experiences, it affects everyone differently. Situations and events that stress out others may not bother you in the least. Some other pertinent facts about stress:

- Nowhere is there more stress experienced than in the workplace.

- Three out of four people (millions!) experience extreme stress at least twice a month.

- There are physical sources of stress (lack of sleep, improper work environment) and psychological sources of stress (fear of losing a job, lack of control and unrealistic work goals).

- Mental fatigue and an overwhelmed immune system drain physical energy and destroy the ability for high productivity when we are under chronic or extreme stress levels for longer than twenty-four hours at a time.

However, small doses of stress can be good for you. To be highly productive, we need the Stress Energy generated by the fight-or-flight hormones our bodies produce when the brain perceives a physically or psychologically stressful situation. This is when our hearts beat faster, our senses sharpen and we're ready to rock 'n roll and get things done! Stress Energy stimulates us and helps us do our best by focusing us on what needs to be accomplished. When properly used, this can turn a stressful situation into a successful outcome.

Since it is impossible to eliminate stress, we need to control our Stress Energy by changing the way our brains respond to stress. This is accomplished by using the following coping techniques:

1: Identify what is causing your stress—your stress triggers (e.g., daily hassles, other people)—then take steps to change the circumstances causing them (i.e., minimize work activities with negative people).

2: Exercise regularly to elevate stress hormones in the body and make the brain and body more resistant to psychological stress.

3: Participate in an activity that gets your mind off work.

4: Get plenty of sleep and eat healthy.

5: Improve Personal Productivity skills.

6: Take a break. Take a walk. Do some quick stretches. Take a day of vacation to re-energize.

7: Laugh. Laughing lightens your load mentally and induces physical changes in your body. It enhances the intake of oxygen-rich air, stimulates your heart, lungs and muscles, increases the endorphins released by your brain and reduces the physical symptoms of stress. By being able to recognize, point out and laugh at the absurdity of unreasonable demands by customers, vendors and co-workers and, at times, our own behavior, we are able to relieve the pressure caused by stress and maintain the level of performance needed to create excellence instead of mediocrity.

8: Approach stressful situations in a more productive fashion. "Self-talk" is the endless stream of positive and negative thoughts running through our heads all the time. These thoughts affect the way we cope with stressful situations. Negative thoughts cause chemical reactions that affect our bodies by bringing more stress into our system. Positive thoughts release neuropeptides that fight stress. By replacing negative thoughts with positive thinking, we develop better stress coping skills.

Rather than fight stress—a losing proposition, since stress is an inherent human survival mechanism—use these techniques and chill out, man!

THE MORNING MANTRA

33

TELECONFERENCING

I Know You're Out There! (The Virtual Meeting)

"A meeting is an event where minutes are taken and hours wasted." —James T. Kirk

More and more business is conducted by long distance methods of communication, such as teleconferencing. While nothing takes the place of face-to-face communication, a teleconference, with advance planning, can be utilized in a very worthwhile way when people can't all be in the same place at the same time.

If you are the Meeting Master (yes, a teleconference is still a meeting, and you don't want it to suck), you will generate the best results with a teleconference by following these basic rules:

1: Only having people on the teleconference who should be there.

2: Giving adequate notice about the time and date of the teleconference.

3: Contacting participants the day before to remind them of the teleconference.

4: Developing a written agenda and sending it to participants in advance of the teleconference.

5: Sending out any materials needed so participants can fully participate.

6: Providing instructions (e.g., specific phone number and call code) on how to participate in the teleconference.

7: Sending reminders of teleconference etiquette (e.g., stating name when speaking, allowing others to complete their statements before speaking, and muting phones when not speaking).

8: Being familiar with the equipment being used.

9: Starting on time.

10: Asking each participant to introduce themselves.

11: Reviewing rules of teleconference etiquette (see #7).

12: Noting everyone's arrival.

13: Keeping participants focused on the agenda items.

14: Not allowing inappropriate language or rudeness.

15: Pausing frequently to give participants time to think and respond.

16: Ending the teleconference on time.

17: Sending out a summary of the teleconference.

18: Asking for participants' feedback by e-mail about how the teleconference went (Was it worthwhile? Did the technology work?) and how the next one can be better.

As with any communication, we only get out of it what we contribute to it. To get the most out of every teleconference, you need to:

a: Be on time.

b: If possible, use a landline phone in a closed room. If you use a cell phone, make sure it is fully charged.

c: Use a headset to minimize background sounds.

d: Permit no interruptions (e.g., phone calls) or distractions, and take an active part in discussions.

e: Get the bathroom break out of the way before the teleconference starts.

f: Know the agenda, meeting materials, etiquette rules and technological requirements.

g: Maintain your focus by keeping your mind on the teleconference and not multitasking (i.e., answering e-mail).

h: Don't speak without identifying yourself.

i: Be courteous. Avoid responding with anger or sarcasm to other participants.

Successful teleconferencing—making sure it doesn't suck—requires adequate preparation and ensuring everyone knows and abides by the rules.

THE MORNING MANTRA

34

TIME MANAGEMENT

Leveraging vs. Managing Time

"Saying 'No' to someone else is like saying 'Yes' to yourself."
—Helene Lerner

On a trip to Fairhope, Alabama (near Mobile), to spend an enjoyable mini-vacation with friends Jackie and Rick (a gourmet cook who caused me to gain seven pounds in four days!), I started thinking about the difference between "leveraging" and "managing" time. Yeah, I know I should really get a life or maybe a Kindle. Regardless, as a productivity junkie, this is a distinction with a difference:

1: Time Leveraging is about being effective, while Time Management is about being efficient;

2: Time Leveraging is about how you invest your time, while Time Management is about how you spend your time.

3: Time Leveraging requires us to ask the question, "Why do we do the things we do?"

4: Time Leveraging is based on the fact time is a limited, non-renewable and non-recoverable resource. This is why it is essential to invest time only in important activities. The definition of an "important activity" is an activity that moves you closer to achieving your Big Hairy Audacious Goals—the ones that really matter. Of course, the first step in Time Leveraging is to determine your BHAG. Then look strategically at how you spend your time by analyzing it (can you say Time Audit?) and determine which activities will move you closer to your BHAG Goals. Then invest time in those activities by developing an Action Plan that establishes how to efficiently do those activities.

5: Without Time Leveraging, Time Management just helps you run faster in the same place.

6: Time Management requires us to ask the question, "How do we do the things we do?"

7: Time Management is based on the self-assessment and planning that results from Time Leveraging.

8: Time Management is about discipline and executing the daily Action Plan to create continual improvement in how you use your time. It is the day-to-day process—the To Do list, delegating, scheduling—that helps you use time efficiently.

This weekend, write down your BHAG. Create an Action Plan dictating when you want to achieve those goals. Then begin to use Time Management to start the journey.

THE MORNING MANTRA

35

OVERCHOICE, TIME POVERTY

"Overchoice" and "Time Poverty"

"Time is the coin of your life. It is the only coin you have, and only you can determine how it will be spent. Be careful lest you let other people spend it for you." —Carl Sandburg

I recently learned two new terms: "Time Poverty" from *The Wizard of Ads*, by Roy Williams; and "Overchoice" from *The 4-Hour Workweek*, by Tim Ferris. These terms stuck with me because they define time problems that plague all of us in the time starved Knowledge Economy.

Overchoice (or "analysis paralysis") is having too many possibilities, too much information and too little time to understand it. This overabundance of information creates inertia that can keep us from accomplishing our goals. To overcome overchoice, we must determine what is important, then focus only on that, and simply ignore the rest. Good advice but extraordinarily difficult to do! However, with practice, this type of strong focus on the essentials can be accomplished since the principle of focus is to exclude, by choice, that which matters less, so we can give our undivided attention to that which matters most. In essence: decreased input = increased output.

Time Poverty is the frustration we feel because we never have enough time to accomplish all our goals. Curiously, it's not the things we do that cause this level of frustration, but the weight of all the things we are *not*

doing. We want more hours in the day to alleviate this situation. Yet we all have the same twenty-four hours each day. Those who are more productive and successful in using their twenty-four hours have avoided Time Poverty by:

1: Focusing on being productive instead of being busy.

2: Eliminating less meaningful work to focus on things of importance.

3: Realizing that doing something unimportant does not make it important.

4: Knowing that just because a task requires a lot of time does not make that task important.

5: Ignoring or redirecting all information/interruptions that are irrelevant, unimportant or un-actionable.

6: Committing to self-discipline. If you cannot make a long-term commitment of time + energy to your Personal Productivity Action Plan, you cannot eliminate Time Poverty.

To overcome Time Poverty and Overchoice, ask yourself the following questions every ninety minutes of each workday: Am I being productive or just active? If this is the only thing I accomplish today, will I be satisfied with my day? If the answers don't make you feel good about how you are spending your time—well, you know what to do.

THE MORNING MANTRA

36

TRAINING

The 72-Hour Rule or He or She Who Hesitates Loses It!

"The key is not in spending time, but in investing it."
—Stephen R. Covey

Nearly everyone has heard of the "five-second rule" (if food falls on the floor and you pick it up within five seconds, you can eat it without cleaning it off). While that rule is expedient, it is clearly wrong. We all know germs don't wait for five seconds to jump on food. Or do they?

However, one rule in which I do believe and explain at the end of every leadership workshop I conduct is the 72-Hour Rule. At the conclusion of a workshop, most participants are full of enthusiasm because they see how implementing the information they received during the workshop will improve their personal and professional lives. But when they return to the pressure cooker of their jobs, they get hit in the face by the reality that they have so much to do and no one to support them as they try to implement a change in the way they perform or behave. Faced with these obstacles, the enthusiasm and good intentions they took from the workshop fade. It becomes easier not to change how they act or perform.

In an effort to prevent this, at the end of each workshop I ask each participant to fill out an individual Action Plan, outlining at least one action they will implement or change immediately. I also take on the role of transitional Accountability Buddy by asking them to contact me on a weekly basis for four weeks to report on the progress they are making in implementing this one change.

However, the most essential item to consider when implementing a new personal improvement change is the 72-Hour Rule. This rule postulates if a person has not started to implement a new change within 72 hours after determining to do so, the odds are it will never be implemented. Why? Because the human mind quickly starts to discard information it is not using. By the end of the fifth day after a workshop, a participant usually only retains 10% of everything presented. However, if a person implements a newly learned concept within 72 hours after being exposed to it, the odds jump to 50% that they will continue to use the new concept. So, when presented with an idea that makes sense to you, implement it immediately—if not sooner—and the odds of it making a positive difference in your life will increase dramatically.

37

TRANSITION

The Transition Period

"We generally change ourselves for one of two reasons: inspiration or desperation." —Jim Rohn

I'm not a golfer. I don't have the patience, and I believe a *real* sport requires a participant to sweat, and not just swear, profusely. However, I view with interest what happens when my golfer friends decide to improve their game, which usually means changing their swing. First, they pay a golf professional, who shows them exactly what they need to do to change their swing and improve their game. Then they play with the new swing and their game sucks. Their frustration and anxiety level rises as their friends make jokes about their bad play. And, though they have invested money and time in acquiring the necessary skill set to improve their game, after a few rounds of frustrating performance, they revert back to their old comfortable swing, which requires no thought or effort, and their game gets no better! I see this pattern occur repeatedly! Why do they engage in this recurring futile process? Because my friends fail to recognize the existence of The Transition Period—the length of time and the amount of effort and energy required to eliminate a bad habit and replace it with a new habit. The trick to developing new Personal Productivity habits that become permanent is discovering how to more easily navigate The Transition Period.

In *Nudge: Improving Decisions About Health, Wealth, and Happiness*, Richard Thaler and Cass Sunstein state that 90% of what we do daily is automatic—based on established habits—and done without much, if any, thought. If we have to think about doing something every time we do it, we won't keep doing it very long—it takes too much effort and energy. To develop new and better Personal Productivity habits, we must make them our "the default options"—the things we automatically do without thinking about them.

How to navigate The Transition Period while developing good replacement habits and get to "the default option" stage is set forth in a *New York Times* article entitled *Can You Become a Creature of New Habits*? The article posits we live in Three Zones: Comfort, Stretch and Stress. "Comfort" is existing habits. We experience the "Stress Zone" when a change in our habits is so great, we cannot envision doing it successfully—therefore, we don't even try to make the change. "Stretch" occurs where, even though a change in our habits may feel odd, it is not so strange it ignites the fight-or-flight reaction we experience when faced with fear of failure (I add a third option: freeze—the "deer-in-the-headlight" posture where we do absolutely nothing and are run over). Successfully changing our Personal Productivity habits, requires we be in the Stretch Zone, and engage in continuous incremental change (check e-mails every 30 minutes instead of every time the "ding" sounds). These continuous incremental changes must be big enough to move us through The Transition Period but be small enough to avoid the Stress Zone (when the thought of only checking e-mails twice a day causes panic to set in).

This incremental approach to changing habits is essential for developing new habits. While a sense of discomfort exists as the Comfort Zone is stretched, if the change process is repeated enough during The Transition Period, your brain creates new synaptic connections that turn your new habit into your "default option." Unfortunately, there is no set length of time for the Transition Period, and the amount of effort and energy it takes to bridge a Transition Period depends on how deeply ingrained the habit being replaced is (ask a smoker the length of The Transition Period to becoming a non-smoker, and they'll tell you it never ends!).

The great thing is, when you have the necessary discipline and determination to endure The Transition Period, you not only replace a bad habit (e.g., answering every e-mail as soon as it arrives) with a good habit (bunching e-mails and answering them every two hours), you also turn the new habit into a routine and—presto! change-o!—you do it without needing to think about it. Your life will be better because you are automatically more productive without any additional expenditure of energy. Try it. All you have to lose is a bad habit.

THE MORNING MANTRA

Final Thought

"Th-Th-Tha-That's NOT All Folks!"
—paraphrasing a very famous pig

This collection of reminders, observations and recommendations is certainly not all you and your organization need to know to survive the WorkQuake™ and thrive in the Knowledge Economy. But it is a good start. If you want to know more about what you and your organization need to do, or just to share your own reminders, observations and recommendations, contact me at paulglover@workquake.com. And I will respond.

P.S.#1: As a bonus for showing me some love by buying my book, visit www.workquake.com and sign up for **Paul's Point of the Day**—a daily dose of WorkQuake™ Wisdom delivered to your computer, iPad, iPhone, etc., six days a week! **And, because you bought my book, it's free!** OMG! By buying my book you actually are getting a rare threefer: **The Bottom Lines, The Morning Mantras** and now **Paul's Points of the Day!** All for a measly few dollars!

P.S.#2: For those who need their daily dose of WorkQuake™ Wisdom in written form, the desk calendar **"365 Days of WorkQuake™ Wisdom"** is available at www.workquake.com.

(This one will cost you a little extra—printing, mailing and all that Industrial Age stuff!)

In 1992, after a thirty-year career as a labor/employment law attorney, Paul Glover founded The Glover Group, a Management Consulting firm dedicated to assisting Companies survive the WorkQuake™ of the Knowledge Economy by improving workplace performance. Paul has a Bachelor of Arts in English from DePaul University, a Masters of Labor Law from Chicago Kent Law School, and a Juris Doctorate Degree from DePaul University's College of Law. Paul is a *FastCompany.com* subject matter expert blogger who teaches Leadership Theory, Assessing Leadership Skills, Communication Skills for Managers, Team Building, Critial Thinking, and Employment Law at National Louis University, Lewis University, and the University of St. Francis.

I hope you enjoyed and got something of value out of the book! If not, go back to page viii.

I can be contacted for speaking engagements and business and executive coaching—or if you just want to chat with me about the WorkQuake™—by email at paulglover@workquake.com or paulglover@trainingeverydayleaders.com. Hope to hear from you soon!